133.4

W9-BDZ-378

t - Europe

European Witchcraft

50

MAJOR ISSUES IN HISTORY

Editor
C. WARREN HOLLISTER,
University of California, Santa Barbara

European Witchcraft

E. William Monter

DEPARTMENT OF HISTORY
NORTHWESTERN UNIVERSITY

John Wiley & Sons, Inc.
New York   London   Sydney   Toronto

Library of Congress Catalogue Card Number: 76-89682

SBN 471 61401 7 (Cloth)   SBN 471 61402 5 (paper)

Printed in the United States of America

PREFACE

Ever since the age of Sir Walter Scott and his *Letters on Demonology*, the subject of European witchcraft appears to be dominated by some form of romantic fallacy. To a twentieth-century American, the mental image conjured up by the word "witch" is likely to be something out of Walt Disney: an old crone in a peaked hat, accompanied by her cat, flying around on a broomstick pointing her long, skinny finger at her intended victim. It may be a more innocuous version, concocted by television; or something out of Roman Polanski, cinematic dabbler in vampires and witches who move in a world of ambiguous realism. Or, if memory is literary instead of visual, it will produce witches à la *MacBeth*, stirring their brew. The common element in all these images is that they were produced by men who, in the last analysis, did not themselves believe in the reality of witchcraft.

With very few exceptions, the modern world has lost the fear of witches and has transformed them into generally harmless creatures capable at most of frightening children. Thus, European witchcraft is a lost historical reality that can only be recaptured by a fresh effort of the imagination. This effort is worth making, for the modern world has not forgotten about witches after losing its fears of them. We have, for example, retained the notion of "witch-trial" while giving it a political context; this may provide the best point of departure for anyone who honestly wishes to recapture the full flavor and historical significance of old-fashioned witchcraft. A "witch-trial" is the result of a genuine public fright, and its prosecutors argue that the suspected crime is so serious that massive and brutal repression is a public service; sparing the innocent is less important than convicting the guilty. But why are "witch-trials" distinguished by precisely this form of judicial cruelty? What was the witch's crime, or crimes, which could produce such mass anxiety?

The literature on European witchcraft provides few convincing answers to these questions. Indeed, it seems to lie under a special curse that condemns its specialists to become slightly infected by the forms of lunacy they set out to describe. One of the most common types of victim is the rationalist fanatic, admirably exemplified by the compiler of a recent *Encyclopedia of Witchcraft and Demonology:* [1]

"For three centuries, from 1450 to 1750, Europe suffered the shocking nightmare, the foulest crime and deepest shame of western civilization, the blackout of everything that *homo sapiens*, the reasoning man, has ever upheld. This book is about that crime and shame.

"The record of witchcraft is horrible and brutal: degradation stifled decency, the filthiest passions masqueraded under cover of religion, and man's intellect was subverted to condone brutalities that even Swift's Yahoos would blush to commit.

"Never were so many so wrong, so long."

And, in direct dialectical opposition to this kind of sensationalist muckraker is the modern occultist, admirably represented by yet another specialist in English literature: [2]

"The rationalist historian and the skeptic, when confronted with the subject of Witchcraft, chose a charmingly easy way to deal with these intensely complex and intricate problems: a flat denial of all statements which did not fit . . with their own narrow prejudice . . . . . Such things could not be. We must argue from that axiom, and therefore anything which it is impossible to explain away by hallucination, or hysteria, or auto-suggestion, or any other vague catchword which may chance to be fashionable at the moment, must be uncompromisingly rejected . . . . Why ex-

[1] Rossell H. Robbins, *Encyclopedia of Witchcraft and Demonology*, New York: Crown, 1959, p. 3.
[2] Montague Summers, *The History of Witchcraft*, New Hyde Park: University Books, 1956; first ed., 1929, p. 3.

amine the evidence? It is really useless and a waste of time . . .
How so absolute and entire falsity of these facts can be demonstrated the skeptic omits to inform us, but we must unquestioningly accept his infallible authority."

Naturally, this does not exhaust the major categories of fanati-
cisms on this subject. There is also, for example, the British gentle-
man-historian who opens his book by remarking naively that "I
have no axe to grind, and am neither a theologian, an occultist,
nor a materialist," but goes on to propose that Robin Hood was
the Devil-king of the fairies and that the Order of the Garter was
somehow connected to the witch-cult because it consisted of two
groups of thirteen people.[3]

Are there serious writers on European witchcraft, capable of
offering an unbiased narrative of what happened? Very few. We
possess many solid antiquarian monographs on the history of the
repression of witchcraft in various parts of Europe, many of them
classifiable as legal history or folklore. But in all of it there is a
good deal of confusion about what witchcraft actually was, and
no agreement on elementary definitions: Was it a mass delusion
foisted upon Christendom by the Church? A secret conspiracy of
giant dimensions, a society of Devil-worshippers? A pagan survival, a fertility cult?

Let us propose some simple definitions. European witchcraft,
as we encounter it between 1450 and 1750, was conceived of as a
virulent and dangerous blend of sorcery and heresy. Sorcery is a
generalized anthropological concept that is almost universal; this
links witchcraft to voodoo, to the black magic of Greco-Roman
antiquity, to African or American Indian or aborigine magic, to
anything that aims at negative supernatural effects through formulas and rituals. The other element, heresy, is the specifically
Christian contribution to the concept of witchcraft; it is the pact
with the Devil, the Witches' Sabbath in the form of a black or
inverted Mass, the new name to replace the Christian name of
baptism. Both ingredients offer important clues as to why witch-

---

[3] Pennethorne Hughes, *Witchcraft*, Baltimore: Penguin Books, 1965, pp.
18, 79, 109.

craft was such a feared and hated crime in Europe. Sorcery, by general agreement, can cause illness in man or beast, even death in extreme cases; it can cause bad weather, destroy fertility in plants or in humans. All these were criminal offenses, which were conveniently united in the idea of witches' *maleficia* or evil spells.

Heresy was also a criminal offense. Christian Europe had forcibly repressed heresies even before the Inquisition was founded, and the notion that heretics ought to be punished was seldom challenged in Europe until the seventeenth century, when it very slowly began to be replaced by the idea that toleration of religious deviants was possible. Yet witchcraft was a special kind of apostasy, more perverse even than conversion to Islam. A witch renounced baptism, salvation, Christ, the sacraments—everything of real importance to a Christian—and served the Devil in person.

It is fairly certain that both heresy and sorcery existed in medieval Europe; at any rate, both were condemned by an impressive number of laws. The masterpiece of witchcraft theory was to combine them, to make sorcery a consequence of a certain kind of heresy, and thereby to create a double crime whose sides were equally horrifying and reprehensible. This dual nature helps explain why witchcraft was regarded as a peculiarly terrible thing— *crimen exceptum*, said the judges—the sort of crime whose repression was so imperative that the end justified any means: torture, false promises, no benefit of doubt . . . any means at all, just so the guilty could be discovered and punished.

What linked sorcery and heresy together in witchcraft theory was the presence of the Devil. Nearly all the great definitions of witchcraft pivot around this point. In 1580, Jean Bodin defined a witch as "someone who knowingly tries to bring about some act through diabolical means." In 1593, the Jesuit Martin Delrio defined witchcraft as "an art by which, through the power of a contract with the Devil, wonders are wrought which pass human understanding." In 1653, the Anglican judge Robert Filmer put it in almost exactly the same words, and the great legal guide, Blackstone, still defined witchcraft in essentially the same terms in the 1730's. It seems to have been generally accepted that the witch or sorcerer received her power from this pact with the

Devil, and that the Devil indeed possessed the ability to cast these evil spells.

This is one more reason why the original concept of witchcraft is so difficult to reconstruct in the contemporary world. Ever since the Enlightenment, we have lived in a post-diabolical world. As Baudelaire said in the nineteenth century, "it is harder for men of this age to believe in the Devil than to love him." And Ivan Karamazov's devil claimed that a newspaper editor had advised him to write anonymously, because the Devil no longer exists. If the average twentieth-century American has a mental picture of a witch, he probably does not have one of the Devil. Yet the witch is logically incomplete without the Devil; witchcraft is the Devil's work, and the witch is the junior partner in this process. No Devil, no witch.

I wish to thank the staff of John Wiley and Sons for their rapid and efficient aid in readying this work for publication. Erik Midelfort of Stanford University perused it carefully and sympathetically, catching several serious errors of fact and interpretation. My wife has scrutinized the numerous translations and introductions in an heroic effort to make my style more correct and easier to read. Dr. John H. Heldt and Robert Wagoner of New York State Maritime College have relieved me of a significant share of the burden of making translations. Naturally, I alone remain responsible for whatever errors of fact and infelicities of style remain.

E. William Monter

Evanston, Illinois
February 1969

SERIES PREFACE

The reading program in a history survey course traditionally has consisted of a large two-volume textbook and, perhaps, a book of readings. This simple reading program requires few decisions and little imagination on the instructor's part, and tends to encourage in the student the virtue of careful memorization. Such programs are by no means things of the past, but they certainly do not represent the wave of the future.

The reading program in survey courses at many colleges and universities today is far more complex. At the risk of oversimplification, and allowing for many exceptions and overlaps, it can be divided into four categories: (1) textbook, (2) original source readings, (3) specialized historical essays and interpretive studies, and (4) historical problems.

After obtaining an overview of the course subject matter (textbook), sampling the original sources, and being exposed to selective examples of excellent modern historical writing (historical essays), the student can turn to the crucial task of weighing various possible interpretations of major historical issues. It is at this point that memory gives way to creative critical thought. The "problems approach," in other words, is the intellectual climax of a thoughtfully conceived reading program and is, indeed, the most characteristic of all approaches to historical pedagogy among the newer generation of college and university teachers.

The historical problems books currently available are many and varied. Why add to this information explosion? Because the Wiley Major Issues Series constitutes an endeavor to produce something new that will respond to pedagogical needs thus far unmet. First, it is a series of individual volumes—one per problem. Many good teachers would much prefer to select their own historical issues rather than be tied to an inflexible sequence of issues imposed by a publisher and bound together between two covers. Second, the Wiley Major Issues Series is based on the idea of approaching the significant problems of history through a deft interweaving of primary sources and secondary analysis, fused together by the skill of a scholar-editor. It is felt that the essence of a historical issue cannot be satisfactorily probed either by placing a body of undigested source materials into the hands of inexperienced students or by limiting these students to the controversial literature of modern scholars who debate the meaning of sources the student never sees. This series approaches historical problems by exposing students to both the finest historical thinking on the issue and some of the evidence on which this thinking is based. This synthetic approach should prove far more fruitful than either the raw-source approach or the exclusively second-hand approach, for it combines the advantages—and avoids the serious disadvantages—of both.

Finally, the editors of the individual volumes in the Major Issues Series have been chosen from among the ablest scholars in their fields. Rather than faceless referees, they are historians who know their issues from the inside and, in most instances, have themselves contributed significantly to the relevant scholarly literature. It has been the editorial policy of this series to permit the editor-scholars of the individual volumes the widest possible latitude both in formulating their topics and in organizing their materials. Their scholarly competence has been unquestioningly respected; they have been encouraged to approach the problems as they see fit. The titles and themes of the series volumes have been suggested in nearly every case by the scholar-editors themselves. The criteria have been (1) that the issue be of relevance to undergraduate lecture courses in history, and (2) that it be an issue which the scholar-editor knows thoroughly and in which he has done creative work. And, in general, the second criterion has been given precedence over the first. In short, the question "What are the significant historical issues today?" has been answered not by general editors or sales departments but by the scholar-teachers who are responsible for these volumes.

University of California,
Santa Barbara

C. Warren Hollister

CONTENTS

Contents

PART ONE

The Origins of Organized Witchcraft

Much of the literature about the origins of witchcraft in Europe is noteworthy for its eccentricity. There is a broad measure of scholarly consensus on two important points: first, that there was remarkably little persecution of witches and magicians during the earlier Middle Ages, with a particularly notable decline around the ninth and tenth centuries (which are otherwise among the "darkest" of the dark ages); second, that by the end of the fifteenth century, during the Renaissance, the legal and theological crime of witchcraft had been molded into finished form. However, the process of this transformation has proved easier to describe (it has been admirably narrated by Joseph Hansen in the first selection) than to explain. At least three major hypotheses have been offered for the emergence of organized witchcraft in Europe all propounded by distinguished scholars. Earliest in the field was the romantic historian Jules Michelet, whose study of La sorcière was published in 1862. He saw historical witchcraft as the consequence of the long "age of despair" in medieval Europe; it was a form of serf response to the otherwise unbearable despair of their condition, a sort of "communion of revolt" acted out at night against the lord of the manor and his church. Michelet believed that witchcraft objectively existed in the Middle Ages, and was already in its decadence when the great persecutions first began during the fifteenth century.

The rationalist and positivist generation at the end of the nineteenth century reacted against such romantic notions. Nearly all the great scholars who dealt with witchcraft between 1870 and 1914 were *firmly skeptical about the historical reality of witchcraft present or past. Consequently they patiently dissected the origins of this delusion, explaining how foolish schoolmen with inadequate epistemological guidelines accepted a lot of gross superstitions and somehow glued them together into one giant folly. They were describing the history of a mass delusion, an imaginary heresy, one of the greatest that had ever gripped Europe, but which was now dead forever.*

The single most influential account of the beginnings of European witchcraft written in the postwar twentieth century reacted against this rationalist approach. Margaret Alice Murray, noted Egyptologist, published The Witch-Cult in Western Europe *in 1921, and continued to defend her position in* The God of the Witches *in 1933. Her central thesis was that "ritual" (as opposed to "operational" or black-magic) witchcraft was actually the survival in Christian Europe of a very ancient fertility cult: the worship of Diana. Margaret Murray's witches were peasants who were falsely accused of harming people through magical practices but who were truly guilty of heresy. They were remnants of the Druidic "little people," also known as elves or fairies, who organized their cult in groups of twelve women and one man. Her opinions finally found their way into the* Encyclopedia Britannica.

Thus far, the controversy over the "real" origins of witchcraft is a classical illustration of a historical debate that generates large amounts of heat but very little light. We know something about how the theory of witchcraft was assembled in late medieval Europe, but very little about what it was assembled from. We understand the process, but we have no idea whether the ingredients were "real." In this sense, the origins of European witchcraft remains an open question.

1 FROM

Zauberwahn, Inquisition und Hexenprozess im Mittelalter

Hansen was a liberal-minded, anticlerical archivist in the Rhineland in the prewar German Empire. His massive and painstaking researches into the origins of witchcraft in Europe finally blossomed into two giant monographs—one an analytic narrative of his subject, the other a richly annotated collection of sources. Hansen's central argument is that the Inquisition, abetted by scholasticism, created "witchcraft" as an organized doctrine during the later Middle Ages. He chose the period 1230-1430 as the critical phase when magical fantasies began to be assimilated into preexisting types of religious heresy. The new theory was perfected and put into practice during the fifteenth century, when the persecutions increased.

Hansen's argument, based on remarkably thorough and meticulous scholarship, remains indispensable to students of the origins of European witchcraft. In fact, it left only two great questions unanswered: first, how much did the Inquisitors and schoolmen invent and how much did they discover in creating their synthesis? (Hansen assumes that it was virtually all invention, and the rest is hidden in the "deep darkness which envelops the ancient history of the human race.") Second, if the witch-craze reached what Hansen calls its final form well before 1500, why did it survive and grow in intensity during the next two centuries, the age of Renaissance and Reformation? (Hansen assumes that this age was "merely the natural decline of the medieval spiritual attitude which was only partially displaced.")

In spite of its great extent and diversity, the literature on witchcraft and witch-persecution offers no adequate answers to show how it was possible during the Christian era, beginning in the fourteenth century, for such a shameful intellectual attitude and disgraceful persecution to develop. The object of our investi-

SOURCE. Joseph Hansen, *Zauberwahn, Inquisition und Hexenprozess in Mittelalter*, Munich: R. Oldenbourg, Verlag, 1900, pp. 4–9 and 31–36. Translated by J. H. Heldt. Reprinted by permission of publisher.

gation is to fill this scholarly void and to clarify the genesis of this persecution, to investigate its scope, its causes and its supporters. We will not concern ourselves with the source of the ideas which constituted this aberration. To do that, we would have to descend into the deep darkness which envelops the ancient history of the human race. Instead, we will confine ourselves essentially to the so-called Middle Ages, without going into the preceding period, and also without going into the frequently-described persecutions of the sixteenth and seventeenth centuries, because they contribute nothing towards the elucidation of our problem. They represent merely the natural decline of the medieval spiritual attitude which was only partially displaced by the Reformation, and which so far as our problem is concerned was practically untouched until far into the modern centuries. This continuation of persecution during the sixteenth century was the natural consequence of a concept propagated during the Middle Ages by the populace and the Church, and deeply engraved with all the power of suggestion into the people's concept of this world. Scholasticism and science connected it to the teachings of the Christian religion and to criminal law, and it was repeatedly given authoritative impact and vitality by teachers and legislators.

All this was already well established at the end of the Middle Ages in the *Malleus Maleficarum*, published in 1486, and in subsequent writings conceived under its influence during the following decades. Nothing of importance was added during later periods which suffered under the burden of their heritage, until the rise of modern philosophy and natural science began to give the world a new intellectual imprint and gave its spirit new, strong wings. What lends a particularly embarrassing and regrettable significance to this development is that the leading powers entrusted with cultural advancement did not remove the elements of this dangerous delusion and the resulting imaginary crimes from the popular mind, but that they imbedded them deeper and deeper, from century to century, with religious zeal. Even today one of these historic powers [the Roman Church] openly includes them in its doctrines. There is probably no more impressive danger signal in the history of the human spirit than the persecution of witches, but the intellectual inertia of theology enables their representatives to bypass it without paying it any attention. Within the framework of today's prevailing religious conceptions, nothing would be more fallacious than to call witchcraft a superstition merely because it no longer plays a role, except in circles that keep alive a liking for things miraculous. Even today it is still a part of Church dogma, and not a superstition in the conventional sense of a relinquished, antiquated and false creed. In order to clarify the development of the delusions with which we are dealing here, it is best to avoid the word "superstition" altogether—a word which is in many respects quite vague. At the present time, of course, a number of the relevant concepts are no longer discussed, even in theological circles. However, even today, they have not really been declared false by those parties, despite the unspeakable misery which they have inflicted upon mankind. The basic concept of this madness—that man, with the aid of demons invoked for that purpose, is able to do harm—is still today part of the recognized teachings of the Catholic Church. As such, it has a definite place in Catholic moral theology. It also possibly (or, rather, probably) has adherents in some Protestant circles.

Since it is our intention to explain the origin of the persecution of witches between 1400 and 1700, we need not include in this discussion the whole immense complex of delusions connected with the Christian belief in demons. We must only deal with those delusions which led to persecutions and which played a part in them. The authors and judges of the fifteenth century, when the extensive persecution began, paint the following picture of the infamous acts committed by the so-called witches—a new sect, they explain, which first arose in their time. They see in them depraved human beings, chiefly women, who made a covenant with the Devil for the purpose of inflicting, with his help and the use of various magic nostrums, all sorts of injuries to their fellow men's body, life, possessions, domestic animals, crops and fruit; human beings who participated in the nocturnal Sabbat presided over by the Devil, who appeared in the flesh and to whom they paid homage; who shamelessly renounced and disgracefully derided Christ, the Church, and the sacraments; who, with the Devil's help, flew swiftly through the air to this Sabbat and to the places of their harmful activities and who committed sexual excesses of the worst kind among themselves and with the Devil; who formed a huge sect of heretics; who, finally, could easily change into animals, especially wolves, cats, or mice, and who appeared in this form to their fellow humans. If it was demonstrated in court that the accused was guilty of *one* of these crimes, it was automatically assumed that he was also guilty of all the others. Especially, anybody who was convicted in court of having participated in the Sabbat was highly suspect of having practiced harmful magic. Looking at the individual components of the collective acts of witchcraft as presented by theological science and legal practice during the fifteenth century, *i.e.* as a new phenomenon, it will appear from the outset that one is dealing with several groups of conceptions which had always existed separately from each other among Oriental and European cultures. One of them is composed of a number of conceptions of harmful sorcery. Not only has it always been the object of punishment by ecclesiastical powers, but it has also independently set the secular power in motion, whenever its head was dominated by the aforementioned religious concept. The secular powers then usually took over the prosecution for damages, and also often intervened because they felt compelled to punish the religious offenses involved. Intimately interwoven with this concept of "harmful sorcery" appear in that collective term primarily various elements derived from the popular belief in ghosts and from the mysteries of the dream world. In the second place appears the idea of sexual intercourse between humans and demons, of which only the religious aspect is considered a crime. The prosecution of these acts is traceable entirely to the initiative of the Church. Thirdly and last, ideas of heresy were also introduced into this concept. This transfer derived its motive from the assumption, developed by the Church, that sorcery, like heresy, is connected with the worship of alien deities. Therefore we find as the driving force of the persecution a Church whose existence was threatened by the heresies.

It is therefore clear that the fight against sorcery and witchcraft could only be undertaken with the conception of the Universe as represented by the medieval intellectual powers, namely that the Church as well as the State viewed most outgrowths of delusion, handed down and faithfully accepted, as factual reality, and punished their practice and manifestations.

According to the doctrine of the Christian Church, it is possible to practice magic and to practice it successfully. It is only a natural consequence of this doctrine that sorcery is repeatedly attempted, despite all injunctions against it. These attempts only stop when one becomes convinced that they are unrealistic and unfruitful. Performing acts of magic was labelled a heinous sin, a crime against religion which demanded punishment by the Church before both the *Forum Internum* (The Sacrament of Penance) and the *Forum Externum* (a spiritual court). Punishment was mandatory, first of all because the crime indicated the sorcerer's apostasy from God and His Church, and furthermore because, according to the Church's teachings on witchcraft, the crime generally had an injurious or at least an immoral effect, *i.e.* it involved harm to fellow men or excitation of evil passions. After the chaos caused by the collapse of the Roman Empire was unravelled, the secular power in the Germano-Tomanic countries became the authority of the Christian world order. Because its conception of sorcery was guided by the Church's metaphysical doctrine, the secular power was convinced of the reality and effectiveness of sorcery. Since it did not necessarily look at the offences of its citizens from a religious or moral point of view, but originally saw the crimes only as interference with the rights of the two private parties involved, the only standard considered for penal legislation was the damage caused by magic acts. Gradually, however, the secular powers learned to view these crimes as a disturbance of public order; also, as a result of the rapid rise of the Church, it considered itself required to enforce the religious views of the Church. As a consequence, secular penal jurisdiction was invaded by the desire not just to punish the alleged damage done by sorcery, but to repress sorcery as an outrage to religion and, so to speak, as a criminal attitude. This point of view had already found expression in the jurisdiction of the Roman Empire. However, in most places it was lost at first in the confusion caused by the decay of the Empire and the consequent diversity of structure in the primitive Germanic states. Subsequently, however, it revived and gradually prevailed to a greater or lesser degree, depending on the relationship of Church to State. Added to these external circumstances, which necessarily resulted in a gradual increase in persecution, was an important internal process of fermentation, magnifying the disaster. With the revival of scientific life in the twelfth century came a natural human need to work out an accurate conception of the inner context and mechanism of magic acts. Since this concept developed one-sidedly on the basis of the Christian world-view, it naturally, for the purpose of its investigation, made use primarily of those elements which were offered by the Christian cosmology and teachings on demons. It was not sufficient to accept merely a connection of sorcerers with demons, effected by sacrifices and formulas; one drew upon the universally developed and detailed Christian Devil-doctrine and on the useful elements in folklore in order to explain the nefarious magical machinations. Occasionally there appeared doubts of sane, human common sense about the reality of sorcery or the accuracy of scholastic methods of explaining it. This only served to spur zealous and obstinate theologians, occupied with these manifestations, to greater emphasis and further expansion of the official explanations. After the year 1000, the Church's fierce struggle against heresy began, starting with the threatening growth of the new Manichaeism of the Cathars—a religious system which, contrary to Christian doctrine, believed that the principle of evil was the ruling force of the visible world. Furthermore, the Church decided to link the sorcerers, the alleged intimates and servants of Satan, with the heretics in order to find heretical characteristics in their activities and to apply to them the newly established heresy jurisdiction of the Inquisition which, according to the secular heresy laws of the thirteenth century, had the secular arm at its unconditional disposal for the execution of its verdicts. The Inquisition also regularly used torture, which the general opinion of the age considered a means of collecting evidence. This was an infallible method of proving the correctness of the Church's scientific theory of the connection between the sorcerer and the Devil through the confessions of the accused.

It was only another step in this downward progression of intellectual confusion to establish the theory that sorcerers, like most heretics, formed a regular sect. . . . It was inevitable that this cluster of ideas, nurtured in the bosom of the Church and its jurisdiction, should have a most disastrous influence on the development of secular criminal law, and that it constantly produced new reasons for the necessity of immediate, forceful intervention by the secular powers. This disastrous development is fairly uniform within the Romano-Germanic ethnic group because of continuous contact and extensive interchange, and it necessarily led to those insane, epidemic persecutions from 1400 to 1700. The Christian world simply did not have the educational resources to free itself from the belief in the reality of sorcery. On the contrary, it constantly introduced new punishable aspects into the activities of people considered to be sorcerers and thereby increasingly mobilized the judicial apparatus of Church and State against the sorcerers, who were considered to be the vilest offenders against religion, the disgusting intimates of Satan, and simultaneously the most dangerous and cunning enemies of their fellow men.

We must visualize this development as occuring essentially in three phases. Until the beginning of the thirteenth century (we chose the year 1230 as our terminal date) Church and State fought against *maleficia* (harmful magic) in its older, simple form. After 1230, the scholastic community investigated the possibility of a connection between humans and demons in a theoretical fashion. Then, under the aegis of the Popes, the simultaneously-founded Inquisition against heresy made these possibilities real by earmarking magic acts as heresy. In this manner, the disastrous collective term "witchcraft" was created from originally scattered features. By 1430 this process was completed and the concept of a sect of sorcerers and witches gained ground. At the same time, this warped notion was exclusively directed towards women, who had previously been given a larger role in only *some* of the conceptions which were now combined into the collective term. Finally, beginning in the fifteenth century, a special theological and canonical literature on witchcraft buttressed the collective term of "witch" which had already arisen from these earlier developments. This was the basis for systematic persecution and for the countless stakes where the victims of deeply-rooted and religiously-sanctioned madness were condemned to the most painful and merciless death.

We shall discuss this persecution only until the middle of the sixteenth century. Its tenacious life, however, lasted into the eighteenth century, but is self-explanatory from the previous development.

2 FROM

Jakob Sprenger and Heinrich Kramer
Malleus Maleficarum (1486)

This oldest and most successful of all handbooks on European witchcraft is a horrible and fascinating work. It climaxed a sustained investigation into witchcraft during the fifteenth century, when at least a dozen treatises were composed on the subject, most of them by Dominican Inquisitors like Sprenger and Kramer. The Malleus *distinguished itself from these predecessors by its completeness and by its practicality. It advanced slowly, disposing of possible objections along its route, and with a confident logic. The* Malleus *is methodical and carefully buttressed by a wide range of authorities; no doubt these qualities help explain why it went through a dozen editions even before the end of the fifteenth century.*

This selection turns on a major problem in witchcraft, namely the witch's responsibility for the various evils or maleficia, *which are produced with the Devil's help. The basic position of the* Malleus *appears to stand on middle ground: the Devil can perform* maleficia *by himself, without witches, and conversely, women can work certain mysterious spells without the Devil's aid. The authors are even capable of skepticism, as with the origins of Job's afflictions (p. 16). But nonetheless they finally emerge with the damning conclusion that witches and the Devil always do work together to cause* maleficia. *Thus they calmly conclude that witchcraft, "the vilest, most evil, and worst" of all mysterious arts, is truly the crime of the witch herself.*

SOURCE. Jakob Sprenger and Heinrich Kramer, *Malleus Maleficarum* (1486), London: The Hogarth Press, Ltd., 1928, Part I, question 2, pp. 12–21. Edited and translated by Montague Summers. Reprinted by permission of the publisher and Mrs. Marianne Rodker.

If it be in accordance with the Catholic Faith to maintain that
in order to bring about some effect of magic, the devil must
intimately cooperate with the witch, or whether one without the
other, that is to say, the devil without the witch, or conversely,
could produce such an effect?

And the first argument is this: That the devil can bring about
an effect of magic without the co-operation of any witch. So
S. Augustine holds. All things which visibly happen so that they
can be seen, may (it is believed) be the work of the inferior
powers of the air. But bodily ills and ailments are certainly not
invisible, nay rather, they are evident to the senses, therefore
they can be brought about by devils. Moreover, we learn from
the Holy Scriptures of the disasters which fell upon Job, how
fire fell from heaven and striking the sheep and the servants consumed them, and how a violent wind threw down the four corners of a house so that it fell upon his children and slew them all.
The devil by himself without the cooperation of any witches, but
merely by God's permission alone, was able to bring about all
these disasters. Therefore he can certainly do many things which
are often ascribed to the work of witches.

And this is obvious from the account of the seven husbands of
the maiden Sara, whom a devil killed. Moreover, whatever a
superior power is able to do, it is able to do without reference to
a power superior to it, and a superior power can all the more
work without reference to an inferior power. But an inferior
power can cause hailstorms and bring about diseases without
the help of a power greater than itself. For Blessed Albertus Magnus in his work *De passionibus aeris* says that rotten sage, if used
as he explains, and thrown into running water, will arouse most
fearful tempests and storms.

Moreover, it may be said that the devil makes use of a witch,
not because he has need of any such agent, but because he is
seeking the perdition of the witch. We may refer to what Aristotle
says in the 3rd book of his *Ethics*. Evil is a voluntary act which
is proved by the fact that nobody performs an unjust action
merely for the sake of doing an unjust action, and a man who
commits a rape does this for the sake of pleasure, not merely
doing evil for evil's sake. Yet the law punishes those who have
done evil as if they had acted merely for the sake of doing evil.

Therefore if the devil works by means of a witch he is merely employing an instrument; and since an instrument depends upon the will of the person who employs it and does not act of its own free will, therefore the guilt of the action ought not to be laid to the charge of the witch, and in consequence she should not be punished.

But an opposite opinion holds that the devil cannot so easily and readily do harm by himself to mankind, as he can harm them through the instrumentality of witches, although they are his servants. In the first place we may consider the act of generation. But for every act which has an effect upon another some kind of contact must be established, and because the devil, who is a spirit, can have no such actual contact with a human body, since there is nothing common of this kind between them, therefore he uses some human instruments, and upon these he bestows the power of hurting by bodily touch. And many hold this to be proven by the text, and the gloss upon the text, in the 3rd chapter of S. Paul's Epistle to the *Galatians:* O senseless Galatians, who hath bewitched you that you should not obey the truth? And the gloss upon this passage refers to those who have singularly fiery and baleful eyes, who by a mere look can harm others, especially young children. And Avicenna also bears this out, *Naturalium*, Book 3, c. the last, when he says: "Very often the soul may have as much influence upon the body of another to the same extent as it has upon its own body, for such is the influence of the eyes of anyone who by his glance attracts and fascinates another." And the same opinion is maintained by Al-Gazali in the 5th book and 10th c. of his *Physics*. Avicenna also suggests, although he does not put this opinion forward as irrefutable, that the power of the imagination can actually change or seem to change extraneous bodies, in cases where the power of the imagination is too unrestrained; and hence we gather that the power of the imagination is not to be considered as distinct from a man's other sensible powers, since it is common to them all, but to some extent it includes all those other powers. And this is true, because such a power of the imagination can change adjacent bodies, as, for example, when a man is able to walk along some narrow beam which is stretched down the middle of a street. But yet if this beam were suspended over deep water he would not dare to walk along it, because his imagination would most strongly impress upon his mind the idea of falling, and therefore his body and the power of his limbs would obey his imagination, and they would not obey the contrary thereto, that is to say, walking directly and without hesitation. This change may be compared to the influence exercised by the eyes of a person who has such influence, and so a mental change is brought about although there is not any actual and bodily change.

Moreover, if it be argued that such a change is caused by a living body owing to the influence of the mind upon some other living body, this answer may be given. In the presence of a murderer blood flows from the wounds in the corpse of the person he has slain. Therefore without any mental powers bodies can produce wonderful effects, and so a living man if he pass by near the corpse of a murdered man, although he may not be aware of the dead body, is often seized with fear.

Again, there are some things in nature which have certain hidden powers, the reason for which man does not know; such, for example, is the lodestone, which attracts steel and many other such things, which S. Augustine mentions in the 20th book *Of the City of God*.

And so women in order to bring about changes in the bodies of others sometimes make use of certain things, which exceed our knowledge, but this is without any aid from the devil. And because these remedies are mysterious we must not therefore ascribe them to the power of the devil as we should ascribe evil spells wrought by witches.

Moreover, witches use certain images and other strange peri-apts, which they are wont to place under the lintels of the doors of houses, or in those meadows where flocks are herding, or even where men congregate, and thus they cast spells over their victims, who have oft-times been known to die. But because such extraordinary effects can proceed from these images it would appear that the influence of these images is in proportion to the influence of the stars over human bodies, for as natural bodies are influenced by heavenly bodies, so may artificial bodies likewise be thus influenced. But natural bodies may find the benefit of certain secret but good influences. Therefore artificial bodies may receive such influence. Hence it is plain that those who perform works of healing may well perform them by means of such good influences, and this has no connextion at all with any evil power.

Moreover, it would seem that most extraordinary and miraculous events come to pass by the working of the powers of nature. For wonderful and terrible and amazing things happen owing to natural forces. And this S. Gregory points out in his *Second Dialogue*. The Saints perform miracles, sometimes by a prayer, sometimes by their power alone. There are examples of each: S. Peter by praying raised to life Tabitha, who was dead. By rebuking Ananias and Sapphira, who were telling a lie, he slew them without any prayer. Therefore a man by his mental influence can change a material body into another, or he can change such a body from health to sickness and conversely.

Moreover, the human body is nobler than any other body, but because of the passions of the mind the human body changes and becomes hot or cold, as is the case with angry men or men who are afraid: and so an even greater change takes place with regard to the effects of sickness and death, which by their power can greatly change a material body.

But certain objections must be allowed. The influence of the mind cannot make an impression upon any form except by the intervention of some agent, as we have said above. And these are the words of S. Augustine in the book which we have already quoted: It is incredible that the angels who fell from Heaven should be obedient to any material things, for they obey God only. And much less can a man of his natural power bring about extraordinary and evil effects. The answer must be made, there are even to-day many who err greatly on this point, making excuses for witches and laying the whole blame upon the craft of the devil, or ascribing the changes that they work to some natural alteration. These errors may be easily made clear. First, by the description of witches which S. Isidore gives in his *Etymologiae*, c. 9: Witches are so called on account of the blackness of their guilt, that is to say, their deeds are more evil than those of any other malefactors. He continues: They stir up and counfound the elements by the aid of the devil, and arouse terrible hailstorms and tempests. Moreover, he says they distract the minds of men, driving them to madness, insane hatred, and inordinate lusts. Again, he continues, by the terrible influence of their spells alone, as it were by a draught of poison, they can destory life.

And the words of S. Augustine in his book on *The City of God* are very much to the point, for he tells us who magicians and witches really are. Magicians, who are commonly called witches, are thus termed on account to the magnitude of their evil deeds. These are they who by the permission of God disturb the elements, who drive to distraction the minds of men, such as have lost their trust in God, and by the terrible power of their evil spells, without any actual draught or poison, kill human beings. As Lucan says: A mind which has not been corrupted by any noxious drink perishes forspoken by some evil charm. For having summoned devils to their aid they actually dare to heap harms upon mankind, and even to destroy their enemies by their evil spells. And it is certain that in operations of this kind the witch works in close conjunction with the devil. Secondly, punishments are of four kinds: beneficial, hurtful, wrought by witchcraft, and natural. Beneficial punishments are meted out by the ministry of good Angels, just as hurtful punishments proceed from evil spirits. Moses smote Egypt with ten plagues by the ministry of good Angels, and the magicians were only able to perform three of these miracles by the aid of the devil. And the pestilence which fell upon the people for three days because of the sin of David who numbered the people, and the 72,000 men who were slain in one night in the army of Sennacherib, were miracles wrought by the Angels of God, that is, by good Angels who feared God and knew that they were carrying out His commands.

Destructive harm, however, is wrought by the medium of bad angels, at whose hands the children of Israel in the desert were often afflicted. And those harms which are simply evil and nothing more are brought about by the devil, who works through the medium of sorcerers and witches. There are also natural harms which in some manner depend upon the conjunction of heavenly bodies, such as dearth, drought, tempests, and similar effects of nature.

It is obvious that there is a vast difference between all these causes, circumstances, and happenings. For Job was afflicted by the devil with a harmful disease, but this is nothing to the purpose. And if anybody who is too clever and over-curious asks how it was that Job was afflicted with this disease by the devil without the aid of some sorcerer of witch, let him know that he is merely beating the air and not informing himself as to the real truth. For in the time of Job there were no sorcerers and witches, and such abominations were not yet practised. But the providence of God wished that by the example of Job the power of the devil even over good men might be manifested, so that we might learn to be on our guard against Satan, and, moreover, by the example of this holy patriarch the glory of God shines abroad, since nothing happens save what is permitted by God.

With regard to the time at which this evil superstition, witchcraft, appeared, we must first distinguish the worshippers of the devil from those who were merely idolaters. And Vincent of Beauvais in his *Speculum historiale,* quoting many learned authorities, says that he who first practised the arts of magic and of astrology was Zoroaster, who is said to have been Ham the son of Noah. And according to S. Augustine in his book *Of the City of God,* Ham laughed aloud when he was born, and thus showed that he was a servant of the devil, and he, although he was a great and mighty king, was conquered by Ninus the Son of Belus, who built Niniveh, whose reign was the beginning of the kingdom of Assyria in the time of Abraham.

This Ninus, owing to his insane love for his father, when his father was dead, ordered a statue of his father to be made, and whatever criminal took refuge there was free from any punishment which he might have incurred. From this time men began to worship images as though they were gods; but this was after the earliest years of history, for in the very first ages there was no idolatry, since in the earliest times men still preserved some remembrance of the creation of the world, as S. Thomas says, Book 2, question 95, article 4. Or it may have originated with Nembroth, who compelled men to worship fire; and thus in the second age of the world there began Idolatry, which is the first of all superstitions, as Divination is the second, and the Observing of Times and Seasons the third.

The practices of witches are included in the second kind of superstition, which is to say Divination, since they expressly invoke the devil. And there are three kinds of this superstition:— Necromancy, Astrology, or rather Astromancy, the superstitious observation of the stars, and Oneiromancy.

I have explained all this at length that the reader may understand that these evil arts did not suddenly burst upon the world, but rather were developed in the process of time, and therefore it was not impertinent to point out that there were no witches in the days of Job. For as the years went by, as S. Gregory says in his *Moralia*, the knowledge of the Saints grew: and therefore the evil craft of the devil likewise increased. The prophet Isaiah says: The earth is filled with the knowledge of the Lord (xi, 6). And so in this twilight and evening of the world, when sin is flourishing on every side and in every place, when charity is growing cold, the evil of witches and their iniquities superabound.

And since Zoroaster was wholly given up to the magic arts, it was the devil alone who inspired him to study and observe the stars. Very early did sorcerers and witches make compacts with the devil and connive with him to bring harm upon human beings. This is proved in the seventh chapter of Exodus, where the magicians of Pharao by the power of the devil wrought extraordinary wonders, imitating those plagues which Moses had brought upon Egypt by the power of good angels.

Hence follows the Catholic teaching, that in order to bring about evil a witch can and does co-operate with the devil. And any objections to this may briefly be answered thus.

1. In the first place, nobody denies that certain harms and damages which actually and visibly afflict men, animals, the fruits of the earth, and which often come about by the influence of the stars, may yet often be brought about by demons, when God permits them so to act. For as S. Augustine says in the 4th book *Of the City of God*: Demons may make use of both fire and air if God allow them so to do. And a commentator remarks: God punishes by the power of evil angels.

2. From this obviously follows the answer to any objection concerning Job, and to any objections which may be raised to our account of the beginnings of magic in the world.

3. With regard to the fact that rotten sage which is thrown into running water is said to produce some evil effect without the help of the devil, although it may not be wholly disconnected with the influence of certain stars, we would point out that we do not intend to discuss the good or evil influence of the stars, but only witchcraft, and therefore this is beside the point.

4. With regard to the fourth argument, it is certainly true that the devil only employs witches to bring about their bale and destruction. But when it is deduced that they are not to be punished, because they only act as instruments which are moved not by their own volition but at the will and pleasure of the principal and agent, there is a ready answer: For they are human instruments and free agents, and although they have made a compact and a contract with the devil, nevertheless they do enjoy absolute liberty: for, as has been learnt from their own revelations—and I speak of women who have been convicted and burned at the stake and who were compelled to wreak vengeance and evil and damage if they wished to escape punishments and blows inflicted by the devil—yet these women do cooperate with the devil although they are bound to him by that profession by which at first they freely and willingly gave themselves over into his power.

With regard to these other arguments, in which it is proved that certain old women have an occult knowledge which enables them to bring about extraordinary and indeed evil effects without the aid of the devil. It must be understood that from one particular to conclude a universal argument is contrary to all sound reason. And when, as it seems, throughout the whole of the Scriptures no such instance can be found, save where it speaks of the charms and spells old women practise, therefore we must not hence conclude that this is always the case. Moreover, the authorities on these passages leave the matter open to question, that is to say, whether such charms have any efficacy without the co-operation of the devil. These charms or fascinations seem capable of division into three kinds. First, the senses are deluded, and this may truly be done by magic, that is to say, by the power of the devil, if God permit it. And the senses may be enlightened by the power of good angels. Secondly, fascination may bring about a certain glamour and a leading astray, as when the apostle says: Who hath bewitched you? *Galatians* iii, I. In the third place, there may be a certain fascination cast by the eyes over another person, and this may be harmful and bad.

And it is of this fascination that Avicenna and Al-Gazali have spoken; St. Thomas too thus mentions this fascination, Part I, question 117. For he says the mind of a man may be changed by the influence of another mind. And that influence which is exerted over another often proceeds from the eyes, for in the eyes a certain subtle influence may be concentrated. For the eyes direct their glance upon a certain object without taking notice of other things, and although the vision be perfectly clear, yet at the sight of some impurity, such as, for example, a woman during her monthly periods, the eyes will as it were contract a certain impurity. This is what Aristole says in his work *On Sleep and Waking*, and thus if anybody's spirit be inflamed with malice or rage, as is often the case with old women, then their disturbed spirit looks through their eyes, for their countenances are most evil and harmful, and often terrify young children of tender years, who are extremely impressionable. And it may be that this is often natural, permitted by God; on the other hand, it may be that these evil looks are often inspired by the malice of the devil, with whom old witches have made some secret contract.

The next question arises with regard to the influence of the heavenly bodies, and here we find three very common errors, but these will be answered as we proceed to explain other matters.

With regard to operations of witchcraft, we find that some of these may be due to mental influence over others, and in some cases such mental influence might be a good one, but it is the motive which makes it evil.

And there are four principal arguments which are to be objected against those who deny that there are witches, or magical operations, which may be performed at the conjunction of certain planets and stars, and that by the malice of human beings harm may be wrought through fashioning images, through the use of spells, and by the writing of mysterious characters. All theologians and philosophers agree that the heavenly bodies are guided and directed by certain spiritual mediums. But those spirits are superior to our minds and souls, just as the heavenly bodies are superior to other bodies, and therefore they can influence both the mind and body of a man, so that he is persuaded and directed to perform some human act. But in order yet more fully to attempt a solution of these matters, we may consider certain difficulties from a discussion of which we shall yet more clearly arrive at the truth. First, spiritual substances cannot change bodies to some other natural form unless it be through the mediumship of some agent. Therefore, however strong a mental influence may be, it cannot effect any change in a man's mind or disposition. Moreover, several universities, especially that of Paris, have condemned the following article:—That an enchanter is able to cast a camel into a deep ditch merely by directing his gaze upon it. And so this article is condemned, that a corporeal body should obey some spiritual substance if this be understood simply, that is to say, if the obedience entails some actual change or transformation. For in regard to this it is God alone Who is absolutely obeyed. Bearing these points in mind we may soon see how that fascination, or influence of the eyes of which we have spoken, is possible, and in what respects it is not possible. For it is not possible that a man through the natural powers of his mind should direct such power from his eyes that, without the agency of his own body or of some other medium, he should be able to do harm to the body of another man. Nor is it possible that a man through the natural powers of his mind should at his will bring about some change, and by directing this power through the mediumship of his eyes entirely transform the body of a man, upon whom he fixes his gaze, just as his will and pleasure may be.

And therefore in neither of these ways can one man influence and fascinate another, for no man by the natural powers of his mind alone possesses such an extraordinary influence. Therefore, to wish to prove that evil effects can be produced by some natural power is to say that this natural power is the power of the devil, which is very far indeed from the truth.

Nevertheless, we may more clearly set forth how it is possible for a careful gaze to do harm. It may so happen that if a man or a woman gaze steadfastly at some child, the child, owing to its power of sight and power of imagination, may receive some very sensible and direct impression. And an impression of this kind is often accompanied by a bodily change, and since the eyes are one of the tenderest organs of the body, therefore they are very liable to such impressions. Therefore it may well happen that the eyes receive some bad impression and change for the worse, since very often the thoughts of the mind or the motions of the body are particularly impressed upon and shown by the eyes. And so it may happen that some angry and evil gaze, if it has been steadfastly fixed and directed upon a child, may so impress itself upon that child's memory and imagination that it may reflect itself in the gaze of the child, and actual results will follow, as, for example, he may lose his appetite and be unable to take food, he may sicken and fall ill. And sometimes we see that the sight of a man who is suffering from his eyes may cause the eyes of those who gaze upon him to dazzle and feel weak, although to a large extent this is nothing else but the effect of pure imagination. Several other examples of the same sort might be discussed here, but for the sake of conciseness we will not discuss them in any further detail.

All this is borne out by the commentators upon the Psalm, *Qui timent te uidebunt me*. There is a great power in the eyes, and this appears even in natural things. For if a wolf see a man first, the man is struck dumb. Moreover, if a basilisk see a man first its look is fatal; but if he see it first he may be able to kill it; and the reason why the basilisk is able to kill a man by its gaze is because when it sees him, owing to its anger a certain terrible poison is set in motion throughout its body, and this it can dart from its eyes, thus infecting the atmosphere with deadly venom. And thus the man breathes in the air which it has infected and is stupefied and dies. But when the beast is first seen by the man, in a case when the man wishes to kill the basilisk, he furnishes himself with mirrors, and the beast seeing itself in the mirrors darts out poison towards its reflection, but the poison recoils and the animal dies. It does not seem plain, however, why the man who thus kills the basilisk should not die too, and we can only conclude that this is on account of some reason not clearly understood.

So far we have set down our opinions absolutely without prejudice and refraining from any hasty or rash judgment, not deviating from the teachings and writings of the Saints. We conclude, therefore, that the Catholic truth is this, that to bring about these evils which form the subject of discussion, witches and the devil always work together, and that in so far as these matters are concerned one can do nothing without the aid and assistance of the other.

We have already treated of this fascination. And now with reference to the second point, namely, that blood will flow from a corpse in the presence of a murderer. According to the *Speculum naturale* of Vincent of Beauvais, c. 13, the wound is, as it were, influenced by the mind of the murderer, and that wound receives a certain atmosphere which has been impressed by and is permeated with his violence and hatred, and when the murderer draws near, the blood wells up and gushes forth from the corpse. For it would seem that this atmosphere, which was caused and as it were entered the wound owing to the murderer, at his presence is disturbed and greatly moved, and it is owing to this movement that the blood streams out of the dead body. There are some who declare that it is due to some other causes, and they say that this gushing forth of the blood is the voice of the blood crying from the earth against the murderer who is present, and that this is on account of the curse pronounced against the first murderer Cain. And with regard to that horror which a person feels when he is passing near the corpse of a man who has been murdered, although he may not be in any way cognizant of the vicinity of a dead body, this horror is psychic, it infects the atmosphere and conveys a thrill of fear to the mind. But all these explanations, be it noted, do not in any way affect the truth of the evil wrought by witches, since they are all perfectly natural and arise from natural causes.

In the third place, as we have already said above, the operations and rites of witches are placed in that second category of superstition which is called Divination; and of this divination there are three kinds, but the argument does not hold good with reference to the third kind, which belongs to a different species, for witchcraft is not merely any divination, but it is that divination, the operations of which are performed by express and explicit invocations of the devil; and this may be done in very many ways, as by Necromancy, Geomancy, Hydromancy, etc.

Wherefore this divination, which is used when they are working their spells, must be judged to be the height of criminal wickedness, although some have attempted to regard it from another point of view. And they argue thus, that as we do not know the hidden powers of nature, it may be that the witches are merely employing or seeking to employ these hidden powers: assuredly if they are employing the natural powers of natural things to bring about a natural effect, this must be perfectly lawful, as indeed is obvious enough. Or even let us conceive that if they superstitiously employ natural things, as, for example, by writing down certain characters or unknown names of some kind, and that then they use these runes for restoring a person to health, or for inducing friendship, or with some useful end, and not at all for doing any damage or harm, in such cases, it may be granted, I say, that there is no express invocation of demons; nevertheless it cannot be that these spells are employed without a tacit invocation, wherefore all such charms must be judged to be wholly unlawful.

And because these and many other charms like to them may be placed in the third category of superstition, that is to say, idle and vain observing of times and seasons, this is by no means a relevant argument as to the heresy of witches. But of this category, the observing of times and seasons, there are four distinct species: A man may use such observations to acquire certain knowledge: or he may in this way seek to inform himself concerning lucky or unlucky days and things: or he may use sacred words and prayers as a charm with no reference to their meaning: or he may intend and desire to bring about some beneficial change in some body. All this St. Thomas has amply treated in that question where he asks, Whether such observing be lawful, especially if it be to bring about a beneficial change in a body, that is to say, the restoration of persons to health. But when witches observe times and seasons, their practices must be held to belong to the second kind of superstition, and there-fore, in so far as they are concerned, questions concerning this third class are wholly impertinent.

We now proceed to a fourth proposition, inasmuch as from observations of the kind we have discussed certain charts and images are wont to be made, but these are of two separate sorts, which differ entirely one from the other; and these are Astronomi-cal and Necromantic. Now in Necromancy there is always an express and particular invocation of demons, for this craft implies that there has been an express compact and contract with them. Let us therefore only consider Astrology. In Astrology there is no compact, and therefore there is no invocation, unless by chance there be some kind of tacit invocation, since the fig-ures of demons and their names sometimes appear in Astrological charts. And again, Necromantic signs are written under the in-fluence of certain stars in order to counteract the influence and oppositions of other heavenly bodies, and these are inscribed, for signs and characters of this kind are often engraved upon rings, gems, or some other precious metal, but magic signs are en-graved without any reference to the influence of the stars, and often upon any substance, nay, even upon vile and sordid sub-stances, which when buried in certain places bring about damage and harm and disease. But we are discussing charts which are made with reference to the stars. And these Necromantic charts and images have no reference to any heavenly body. Therefore a consideration of them does not enter into the present discussion.

Moreover, many of these images which have been made with superstitious rites have no efficacy at all, that is to say, in so far as the fashioning of them is concerned, although it may be that the material of which they are made does possess a certain power, although this is not due to the fact that they were made under the influence of certain stars. Yet many hold that it is in any case unlawful to make use even of images like these. But the images made by witches have no natural power at all, nor has the material of which they are formed any power; but they fashion such images by command of the devil, that by so doing they may, as it were, mock the work of the Creator, and that they may provoke Him to anger so that in punishment of their misdeeds He may suffer plagues to fall upon the earth. And in order to increase their guilt they delight especially to fashion many such images at the more solemn seasons of the year.

With regard to the fifth point, St. Gregory is there speaking of the power of grace and not of the power of nature. And since, as St. John says, we are born of God, what wonder then that the sons of God enjoy extraordinary powers.

With regard to the last point we will say this, that a mere likeness is irrelevant, because the influence of one's own mind on one's own body is different from its influence upon another body. For since the mind is united to the body as though the body were the material form of the mind, and the emotions are an act of the body, but separate, therefore the emotion can be changed by the influence of the mind whensoever there is some bodily change, heat or cold, or any alteration, even to death itself. But to change the actual body, no act of the mind is sufficient by itself, unless there can be some physical result which alters the body. Whence witches, by the exercise of no natural power, but only by the help of the devil, are able to bring about harmful effects. And the devils themselves can only do this by the use of material objects as their instruments, such as bones, hair, wood, iron, and all sorts of objects of this kind, concerning which operation we shall treat more fully a little later.

Now with regard to the tenor of the Bull of our Most Holy Father the Pope, we will discuss the origin of witches, and how it is that of recent years their works have so multiplied among us. And it must be borne in mind that for this to take place, three things concur, the devil, the witch, and the permission of God who suffers such things to be. For St. Augustine says, that the abomination of witchcraft arose from this foul connection of mankind with the devil. Therefore it is plain that the origin and the increase of theis heresy arises from this foul connexion, a fact which many authors approve.

We must especially observe that this heresy, witchcraft, not only differs from all other heresy in this, that not merely by a tacit compact, but by a compact which is exactly defined and expressed it blasphemes the Creator and endeavours to the utmost to profane Him and to harm His creatures, for all other simple heresies have made no open compact with the devil, no compact, that is, either tacit or exactly expressed, although their errors and misbelief are directly to be attributed to the Father of errors and lies. Moreover, witchcraft differs from all other harmful and mysterious arts in this point, that of all superstition it is essentially the vilest, the most evil and the worst, wherefore it derives its name from doing evil, and from blaspheming the true faith. (*Maleficae dictate a Maleficiendo, seu a malle de fide sentiendo.*)

Let us especially note too that in the practice of this abominable evil, four points in particular are required. First, most profanely to renounce the Catholic Faith, or at any rate to deny certain dogmas of the faith; secondly, to devote themselves body and soul to all evil; thirdly, to offer up unbaptized children to Satan; fourthly, to indulge in every kind of carnal lust with Incubi and Succubi and all manner of filthy delights.

Would to God that we might suppose all this to be untrue and merely imaginary, if only our Holy Mother the Church were free from the leprosy of such abomination. Alas, the judgment of the Apostolic See, who is alone the Mistress and the Teacher of all truth, that judgment, I say, which has been expressed in the Bull of our Holy Father the Pope, assures us and makes us aware that these crimes and evils flourish amongst us, and we dare not refrain from inquiring into them lest we imperil our own salvation. And therefore we must discuss at length the origin and the increase of these abominations; it has been a work of much labour indeed, but we trust that every detail will most exactly and most carefully be weighed by those who read this book, for herein will be found nothing contrary to sound reason, nothing which differs from the words of Scripture and the tradition of the Fathers.

Now there are two circumstances which are certainly very common at the present day, that is to say, the connexion of witches with familiars, Incubi and Succubi, and the horrible sacrifices of small children. Therefore we shall particularly deal with these matters, so that in the first place we shall discuss these demons themselves, secondly, the witches and their works, and thirdly, we will inquire wherefore such things are suffered to be. Now these demons work owing to their influence upon man's mind and upon his free will, and they choose to copulate under the influence of certain stars rather than under the influence of others, for it would seem that at certain times their semen can more easily generate and beget children. Accordingly, we must inquire why the demons should act at the conjunction of certain stars, and what times these are.

There are three chief points to discuss. First, whether these abominable heresies can be multiplied throughout the world by those who give themselves to Incubi and Succubi. Secondly, whether their actions have not a certain extraordinary power when performed under the influence of certain stars. Thirdly, whether this abominable heresy is not widely spread by those who profanely sacrifice children to Satan. Moreover, when we have discussed the second point, before we proceed to the third, we must consider the influence of the stars, and what power they have in acts of witchcraft.

Stop

3 FROM *Hugh Trevor-Roper*
Religion, the Reformation, and Social Change

This recent, lengthy essay by the Regius Professor of Modern History at Oxford ranks among the best general treatments of the history of European witchcraft. Trevor-Roper's central argument, repeated throughout his essay, is that witchcraft must be understood primarily as a manifestation of social conflict: between monastic orders and their superficially Christian flocks in the later Middle Ages, between Protestants and Catholics, and ultimately between lawyers or clergy and educated laymen. His thesis, I believe, applies far better to some parts of his subject than to others.[1] And it is not altogether original, for Joseph Hansen had noticed that the great persecutions of the fifteenth century originated in the Alps and Pyrenees, lands of uncivilized mountaineers, subject to sudden and violent changes of nature and prone to cretinism;[2] but he did not carry this point as far,

[1] For a general critique, see my "Trois historiens actuels de la sorcellerie," in *Bibliothéque d'humanisme et renaissance*, XXXI (1969), pp. 205–13.

[2] Hansen, *Zauberwahn*, pp. 400–01.

or explain it nearly as well as Trevor-Roper has done. The overall value of Trevor-Roper's essay can be seen at many other points in this anthology, particularly in his new insights into the reasons for the decline of persecution in Europe discussed in Part Four.

When Hansen wrote that the system of the new witch-craze had achieved its final form by the 1480s, he was referring to the two documents of that decade from which the centralized European witch-craze, as distinct from spasmodic local outbursts, can be dated. The first of these is the papal bull *Summis Desiderantes Affectibus*, issued by Pope Innocent VIII in December 1484, deploring the spread of witchcraft in Germany and authorizing his beloved sons, the Dominican inquisitors Heinrich Institor (Krämer) and Jakob Sprenger, to extirpate it. The second is the earliest great printed encyclopaedia of demonology, the *Malleus Maleficarum,* "the Hammer of Witches," published by these same two inquisitors two years later, in 1486. The relationship between these two documents is perfectly clear: they are complementary one to the other. The papal bull had been solicited by the inquisitors, who wished for support in their attempt to launch the witch-craze in the Rhineland. Having obtained it, they printed it in their book, as if the book had been written in response to the bull. The book thus advertised to all Europe both the new epidemic of witchcraft and the authority which had been given to them to suppress it.

The importance of the papal bull of 1484 is incontestable. Apologists for the papacy have protested that it made no change: it was merely a routine document which authorized the Dominicans to go on doing what they were already doing and told other authorities—bishops and secular powers—not to obstruct their work. No doubt it did this; but it also did something else, which was new. What the Dominicans had been doing hitherto was

SOURCE. Hugh R. Trevor-Roper, *Religion, the Reformation, and Social Change,* London: Macmillan & Co. Ltd., 1967 pp. 101–108. Published simultaneously in New York by Harper & Row under the title *The Crisis of the Seventeenth Century.* Copyright © 1967 by H. R. Trevor-Roper. Reprinted by permission of the publishers.

local. They had been persecuting and burning witches locally. From now on a general mandate was given, or implied. And the *Malleus*, which is inseparable from the bull, gave force and substance to that mandate. First, by its content, by gathering together all the curiosities and credulities of Alpine peasants and their confessors, it built up a solid basis for the new mythology. Secondly, by its universal circulation, it carried this mythology, as a truth recognized by the Church, over all Christendom. Finally, the *Malleus* explicitly called on other authorities, lay and secular, not merely not to obstruct, but positively to assist the inquisitors in their task of exterminating witches. From now on, the persecution, which had been sporadic, was—at least in theory—made general, and secular authorities were encouraged to use the methods and mythology of the Inquisition. Rome had spoken.

Why did Rome speak? Why did Innocent VIII, that worldly humanist, the patron of Mantegna and Pinturicchio, Perugino and Filippino Lippi, yield to these fanatical Dominican friars? The answer, obviously, is not to be sought in his personality. It is to be sought rather in circumstances: in the historical situation out of which the witch-beliefs had arisen and in the war which the Dominican inquisitors had long been waging against them. This question brings us at once to a particular area, the area in which these beliefs had always been endemic and in which, for two centuries, they had already been persecuted: the mountain areas of Catholic Europe, the Alps and the Pyrenees.

The mountain origin of the witch-craze is by now well established. So are the circumstances in which it was formulated, and in which the Dominicans came to be its great adversaries. These circumstances bring us back to the very foundation of the order, in the struggle between the Catholic Church and the heretics of the twelfth century, the Albigensians of Languedoc and the Vaudois of the Alps. It was to combat these heretics that the Inquisition and the Dominican order had been founded, and it was in the course of that "crusade" that the inquisitors had discovered, beneath the forms of one heresy, the rudiments (as they thought) of another. From an early date, therefore, they had pressed the Pope to grant them jurisdiction over witchcraft as well as over recognized theological heresy. To the Dominicans the two forms of error were inseparable: one continued the other, and the pursuit must not cease when the formal error had disappeared underground. They could still recognize it by its smell. So, although the form might seem to change, the old names persisted. By the fifteenth century we hear little of Vaudois or Cathari as theological terms: those errors had been burnt out, at least for a time. But in the Alps, in the Lyonnais and in Flanders witches are known as *Waudenses* and their gatherings as a *Valdesia* or *Vauderye*, and in the Pyrenees we find them described as *Gazarii* or "*Cathars*."

When the Dominicans pressed for inquisitorial power over witchcraft, the papacy had at first resisted. The old canons of the Church, and particularly the *canon Episcopi*, denied the reality of witches and forbade their persecution. Therefore, in 1257, Pope Alexander IV had refused these demands unless manifest heresy, not merely witchcraft, could be proved. But little by little, under constant pressure, the papacy had yielded. The great surrender had been made by the French popes of Avignon, and particularly by the two popes from southern France, John XXII and his successor Benedict XII, who had already, as bishops in Languedoc, waged war on nonconformity in the old Albigensian and Vaudois areas. John XXII, who declared heretical the Franciscan doctrine of the poverty of Christ (so dangerously akin to the old Vaudois ideas), also, by his constitution *Super illius specula* of 1326, authorized the full use of inquisitorial procedure against witches, of whom he lived in personal terror. For the next century and a half—until the Witch Bull of Innocent VIII, and indeed afterwards—the main effort of the inquisitors (although there were some spectacular "political" witchcraft trials in France, Burgundy and England) had been directed against the witches of the Alps and the Pyrenees.

At first the campaign was most vigorous in the Pyrenees. From the papacy of John XXII onwards, witch-trials were held all over the old Albigensian territory; but soon they spread to the Alps also. The sitting of the Council of the Church in Basel in 1435-1437 gave a great opportunity to the local witch-hunters, and it was in those years that a zealous inquisitor, John Nider, wrote what has been called "the first popular essay on witches." It was called *Formicarius*, "the Ant-heap," and was based principally on confessions of Swiss witches collected by a Swiss magistrate, Peter of Berne. The *Formicarius* may be regarded as a little *Malleus*, and it had a similar effect in a more restricted field. Papal instructions were sent out to the witch-inquisitors to re-double their zeal, and in 1440, the Pope took the opportunity to denounce his rival, "that eldest son of Satan, Amadeus, Duke of Savoy," as having given himself over to the witches "or Vau-dois" who abound in his land. In the next hundred years some famous inquisitors were busy in the Alpine valleys—Bernard of Como, Jerome Visconti, Bartolomeo Spina. In 1485, according to the *Malleus*, the inquisitor of Como burnt forty-one witches, all of whom confessed to sexual intercourse with *incubi*, and yet even so the practice was increasing. This was the point of time at which the Witch Bull and the *Malleus* were published.

Meanwhile the Pyrenean inquisitors, after a temporary lull, had resumed their activities. In 1450 they too produced a little *Malleus*. This was a tract by Jean Vineti, Dominican inquisitor of Carcassonne: the first work, it seems, to declare that witch-craft was a new heresy, unconnected with the old rural beliefs which the Church of the past had tolerated. This separation of the new witchcraft from the old was a point of great technical im-portance. Indeed, we can say that it gave the witch-craze its charter: for it enabled the inquisitors to get round the greatest obstacle in the way of witch-persecution: the *canon Episcopi*. About the same time witch-beliefs were found to have spread to the Spanish slopes of the Pyrenees and the King of Castile was invited to take action against them.

Thus by the time that the authors of the *Malleus* obtained the blessing of Pope Innocent VIII, the craze had already been in operation for nearly two centuries in the mountain areas, the old homes of heresy and centres of inquisitorial persecution. The two authors of the *Malleus*, the solicitors of the bull, were themselves natives of the Alpine regions, and all their examples and cases are drawn from upper Germany. The most active of the pair was Krämer, who was inquisitor in the Tyrol; he afterwards became inquisitor in Bohemia and Moravia, where he acted vigorously against the "Waldenses" of Bohemia as well as against witches.

The Alps and the Pyrenees, the original cradle of the witch-craze, would long remain its base. Individual witches, of course, might be found anywhere, and in certain circumstances might infect whole areas: for the old unorganized superstitions of the countryside were always there, always ready to be inflamed. Isolated rural societies anywhere—in the dreary flats of the Landes in France, or of Essex in England, or in the sandy plain of north Germany—would always be subject to witch-beliefs. Psychopathic disturbances, which could easily be rationalized as witchcraft, are independent of geography. Individual inquisitors, too, would discover or create beliefs in any area in which they happened to operate: Krämer and Sprenger would have plenty of counterparts among the Protestant clergy—and among the laity too, like Matthew Hopkins, the famous "witch-finder general" of the English civil war. But these are secondary developments, individual extensions. As a continuing social phenomenon, involving not merely individuals but whole societies, the witch-craze would always be associated particularly with the highlands. The great European witch-hunts would centre upon the Alps and their foothills, the Jura and the Vosges, and upon the Pyrenees and their extensions in France and Spain. Switzerland, Franche-Comté, Savoy, Alsace, Lorraine, the Valtelline, the Tyrol, Bavaria and the north Italian bishoprics of Milan, Brescia and Bergamo; Béarn, Navarre and Catalonia: these would be primary centres. Here the new heresy had been discovered, hence it would be generalized. From the fantasies of mountain peasants, the Dominicans elaborated their systematic demonology and enabled or compelled Renaissance popes to denounce a new heresy in Europe. The heads of the old Albigensian and Vaudois heresy were sprouting again.

This prevalence of witchcraft, and of illusions that can be interpreted as witchcraft, in mountainous areas doubtless has a physical explanation. Rural poverty, as Michelet observed, naturally drives men to invoke the spirits of revenge. The thin air of the mountains breeds hallucinations, and the exaggerated phenomena of nature—the electric storms, the avalanches, the cracking and calving of the mountain ice—easily lead men to believe in demonic activity. But these explanations, by themselves, are not enough. Rural poverty, after all, was a commonplace of all centuries. So, no doubt, were some of the beliefs that it engenders. The superstitions of the mountain are but exaggerations of the superstitions of the plain. Why then, we ask, did the Dominicans wage such war on them? Why did they insist on seeing them as something different from the superstitions which, in the plain, the Church had so long tolerated or ignored? What was the underlying, permanent difference which the Dominicans rationalized as successive layers of "heresy"?

Sometimes, no doubt, it was a difference of race. The Basques, for instance, were racially distinct from the latinized Germans—Franks and the Visigoths—around them. But difference of race, though it may sharpen other differences, is not in itself decisive. It is only when it corresponds with difference of social organization that conflict or incompatibility arises; and then it is the social difference which decides. In the Middle Ages the men of the mountains differed from the men of the plains in social organization, and therefore they also differed in those customs and patterns of belief which grow out of social organization and, in the course of centuries, consecrate it. Theirs, we may almost say, were different civilizations.

Medieval civilization, "feudal" civilization, was a civilization of the plains, or at least of the cultivated lands which could sustain the manor and its organization. In the poor mountain areas, pastoral and individualist, this "feudalism" had never fully established itself. Sometimes Christianity itself had hardly penetrated thither, or at least it had not been maintained there in comparable form. Missionaries might have carried the Gospel into the hills, but a settled Church had not institutionalized it, and in those closed societies a lightly rooted orthodoxy was easily turned to heresy or even infidelity. M. Fernand Braudel, in his incomparable work on the Mediterranean, has commented, briefly but brilliantly, on this fact. He has pointed to isolated mountain societies long untouched, or only superficially touched, by the religion of state and easily—if as superficially—converted to the heresy of new evangelists or the religion of a sudden conqueror. The conversion of the mountains to Christianity—or, for that matter, to Islam—(he writes) was far from complete in the sixteenth century; and he refers to the Berbers of the Atlas mountains, and the highland Kurds in Asia, so slowly won for Mohammed, "'while the highlands of Spain will preserve the re-

ligion of the Prophet in Christian Spain and the wild Alps of Lu-
béron protect the lingering faith of the Vaudois."

The mountains, then, are the home not only of sorcery and
witchcraft, but also of primitive religious forms and resistance
to new orthodoxies. Again and again they have to be won back to
sound religion; for missionaries come and go and the established
Church does not easily take root in such poor soil. We see this in
England, where the north and west, "the dark corners of the
realm," would have to be re-evangelized by Puritan missionaries
a century after the Reformation, and in Scotland, where the
Highlands would relapse into "paganism" and would need to be
recovered by a new Puritan movement in the eighteenth century. What would happen in Britain after the Reformation had
happened in Europe before it. The Dominicans were the evangelists of the "dark corners" of Europe where the Catholic Church
was not permanently established. As such they carried the gospel
of "feudal" Christian Europe into the unfeudal, half-Christian societies of the mountains, and inevitably, in that different world,
found that their success was transitory: that ancient habits of
thought reasserted themselves, that social incompatibility clothed
itself in religious heresy, and that when formal heresy had been
silenced or burnt out, the same fundamental incompatibility
took, or seemed to take, another form. The old rural superstition,
which had seemed harmless enough in the interstices of known
society, assumed a more dangerous character when it was discovered, in strange, exaggerated form, among the barely subdued
"heretics" of the highlands. Thanks to that social gulf, that social
unassimilability, witchcraft became heresy.

PART TWO

The Great Witchcraft Debate, 1560-1580

Scholars have long recognized that the great bulk of witchcraft trials in Europe did not follow immediately after the publication of the Malleus Maleficarum, but began almost a full century later—in Elizabethan England, in the France of Henri III, and in most parts of Germany in the later years of the sixteenth century. The first half of that century, the peak period of Renaissance and Reformation in northern Europe, recorded far less persecution of witches than the second half. In many regions of Europe—for example, the area running from Geneva and Savoy north through Vaud, Franche-Comté, Neuchâtel, Montbéliard into Alsace and Lorraine—every province, Protestant and Catholic alike, saw a rapid intensification of persecution beginning sometime between the 1560's and the 1580's.

If the fact of rapidly increasing persecution in the last third of the sixteenth century has been established, its explanation is still very much in doubt. Two important hypotheses have recently been offered, both relying more on social than on intellectual history. The first[1] attempts to establish a rhythm between the persecution of heretics during the wars of religion from 1560 to 1590, and the persecution of witches from 1590 to 1630. It is even possible to find specific examples where witchcraft trials begin precisely at the point where heresy trials stop:

---

[1] Robert Mandrou, *Introduction à la France moderne: essai de psychologie historique*, Paris, 1963, p. 363. Mandrou has a few hesitations when he repeats the same hypothesis in his *Magistrats et sorciers en France au XVIIe siècle*, Paris, 1968, p. 152.

the bishopric of Cologne ceased trials for Anabaptism and started trials for malign sorcery around 1605; the city of Besançon stopped trials of Huguenots and began trials of witches around 1585. But very often witchcraft trials occurred in regions without any traditions of heresy trials, and many regions had had witch-trials long before they had heresy trials of Protestants. Another explanation[2] argues that the increase in persecution was a natural by-product of the wars of religion between Catholic and Protestant, a result of the heat of religious conflict. However, this explanation encounters many of the same difficulties as the other, since the upsurge of witchcraft persecution often lacked any geographical or chronological connection with the religious wars. In fact, regions that actually experienced such wars generally stopped their witchcraft trials for a long time, because their general judicial machinery was likely to have been badly damaged by these wars.

Perhaps a better set of explanations can be uncovered if we look at some simple facts of sixteenth-century European intellectual history. First, both the Protestant and Catholic reformations can best be understood as different aspects of the same spirit of religious revival, rather than as a social conflict. Because the persecution of heretics is a valuable index of the depth of religious zeal, and because witchcraft was the very worst sort of anti-Christian heresy—an organized sect of Devil-worshippers—it is not difficult to understand this enormous outburst of persecution as merely one disastrous consequence of this general eruption of religious zeal.

In order to establish such a line of argument, it is also necessary to show that both Catholic and Protestant educated opinion had no serious cause to doubt either the reality of witchcraft and its crimes or the necessity of its abolition. The argument of this section, expounded most fully in the final essay, is that there was no natural explanation for witchcraft that could stand up under serious sixteenth-century criticism. There was a great polemical debate about the reality of witchcraft and the persecution of witches in the later sixteenth century, a debate that cut across confessional lines. Johann Weyer launched it by attacking witchcraft in the 1560's, and Jean Bodin concluded it with a defense of witchcraft in 1580.

[2] Hugh Trevor-Roper, Religion, the Reformation, and Social Change, London and New York, 1967, p. 139ff.

1 FROM *Johann Weyer*
De Praestigiis Daemonum (1563)

A disciple of the famous Renaissance physician Cornelius Agrippa—who later served as a model for Dr. Faustus—Weyer spent most of his adult life (1550-1578) as court physician to the tolerant, Erasmian Duke of Cleves. His book on the illusions and impostures of devils, his frontal attack on the witchcraft belief and persecution, was the masterpiece of his life. It had four Latin editions from 1563-1568, was translated into German and French in 1567, was reprinted in an enlarged Latin edition in 1577, and this newer version was also translated into French in 1579. This is a very respectable record, considering the boldness of some of Weyer's claims about witches.

De Praestigiis Daemonum is a long book, forever interrupting its argument with more or less relevant disgressions. Weyer's central theme, which he clearly suggests in his preface, is that witches are really harmless and confused old women, suffering from various physical and mental disorders; he insists that natural, medical explanations can be found for nearly all cases of presumed witchcraft, and that the exceptions result from poison rather than black magic. The chapters translated here are not the very best of Weyer, but they do concern a central point of witchcraft, namely the nature of the pact between witches and the Devil. Weyer argues that such pacts are legally frauds, and that witches' brews and unguents do not contain any magical properties. Note also that he argues as a Protestant, especially when discussing witches' crimes against Church ceremonies.

SOURCE. Johann Weyer, *De Praestigüs Daemonum* (1563) Book III, chapters iii-iv and translated from E. Bourneville, ed. *Histoire, Disputes et Descours des Illusions et Impostures des Diables, etc.*, Paris, 1885. Vol. I, pp. 285-296. Dedicatory epistle to Duke William of Cleves reprinted from pp. 213-215 of *A History of Medical Psychology* by Gregory Zilboorg, M.D. in collaboration with George W. Henry, M.D. By permission of W.W. Norton & Company, Inc. Copyright 1941 by W.W. Norton & Company, Inc. Copyright renewed 1968 by Margaret Stone Zilboorg and George W. Henry.

PREFACE

Of all the misfortunes which the various fanatical and corrupt opinions, through Satan's help, have brought in our time to Christendom, not the smallest is that which, under the name of witchcraft, is sown as a vicious seed. The people may be divided against themselves through their many disputes about the Scriptures and church customs, while the old snake stirs the fire; still no such great misfortune results from that as from the thereby inspired opinion that childish old hags whom one calls witches or sorcerers can do any harm to men and animals. Daily experience teaches us what cursed apostasy, what friendship with the wicked one, what hatred and strife among fellow creatures, what dissension in city and in country, what numerous murders of innocent people through the devil's wretched aid, such belief in the power of witches brings forth. No one can more correctly judge about these things than we physicians whose ears and hearts are being constantly tortured by this superstition.

I notice more from day to day that the bog of Camarina blows its plague-laden breath stronger than ever. For a time one hoped that its poison would be gradually eliminated through the healthy teaching of the word of God, but I see that in these stormy days it reaches farther and farther and wider than ever. In the same way the sly devil watchfully uses each propitious circumstance. In the meantime the priests sleepily allow him to continue. Almost all the theologians are silent regarding their godlessness, doctors tolerate it, jurists treat it while still under the influence of old prejudices; wherever I listen, there is no one, no one who out of compassion for humanity unseals the labyrinth or extends a hand to heal the deadly wound.

Therefore I, with my limited means, have undertaken to challenge the grievous thing which disgraces our Christian faith. It is not arrogance which impels me. I know that I know nothing and that my work allows me little leisure. I know too that many others could do this work better than I. I would like to incite them to outdo me. I shall gladly listen to reason.

My object is chiefly of a theological nature: to set forth the artfulness of Satan according to Biblical authority and to demonstrate how one can overcome it. Next, my object is philosophical, in that I fight with natural reason against the deceptions which proceed from Satan and the mad imagination of the so-called witches. My object is also medical, in that I show that those illnesses the origin of which is attributed to witches come from natural causes. And finally, my object is legal, in that I speak of the punishment, in another than the accustomed way, of sorcerers and witches.

But in order that I shall not meet with the reproach that I have overstepped the boundaries of my intellectual power and the limits of my profession with too great a faith in my own intelligence, I have submitted my seemingly paradoxical manuscript to men of your Highness' family as well as to theologians, lawyers, and excellent physicians, that it may be read in a critical sense. The manuscript shall remain protected through their authority if it is founded on reason; it shall fall if it is judged to be in error; it shall become better if it needs supplement or revision. For there is nothing in the world which can be made immediately and at once completely perfect.

One might rejoin here that the *Malleus Maleficarum* has already fulfilled this mission. But one has only to read in that book the silly and often godless absurdities of the theologians Heinrich Kraemer and Jacob [Johann] Sprenger and to compare these quietly with the content of my manuscript. Then it will be clearly seen that I expound and advocate a totally different, even an opposite, point of view.

To you, Prince, I dedicate the fruit of my thought. For thirteen years your physician, I have heard expressed in your Court the most varied opinions concerning witches; but none so agrees with my own as does yours, that witches can harm no one through the most malicious will or the ugliest exorcism, that rather their imagination—inflamed by the demons in a way not understandable to us—and the torture of melancholy makes them only fancy that they have caused all sorts of evil. For when the entire manner of action is laid on the scales, and the implements therefor examined with care and scrutiny, the nonsense and falsity of the matter is soon clear to all eyes and more lucid than the day. You do not, like others, impose heavy penalties on perplexed, poor old women. You demand evidence, and only if they have actually given poison bringing about the death of men or animals do you allow the law to take its course.

When a prince of such virtues protects me, I have faith that I can make short work of the snapping teeth of insolent quarrelers, especially since it is certain that on my side stands invincible truth. I implore God, the Highest and Best, the Father of our Lord Jesus Christ, that He may profitably extend through greater employment of the Holy Spirit what in His benevolence He has so happily begun in Your Highness, to the honor of His Name, to the glory of Your Highness and to the flourishing happiness of your country. Your Highness' most obedient servant, Johann Weyer, Physician.

CHAPTER III: THE CLAIMS OF THE WITCHES UNMASKED AND REFUTED: SHOWING THAT THEIR PACT AND AGREEMENT IS ONLY AN IMPOSTURE, AND MADNESS, WHICH SHOULD BE DISREGARDED

Any man who is not completely dull-witted will easily conclude that these things are mutually contradictory, absurd, and unworthy of belief. He will also easily know that the pact [with the Devil] is only an imposture made by the appearance of some imaginary phantom or fantastic body, and grasped by a dazzled mind; or else made by some trick played on the optical nerves, by a figure concocted and adapted by Satan to the humors and spirits moving in this region. Else it is made and fixed by a breeze or dull sound or murmur in the organs of hearing, corresponding to and agreeing with the figures of the deceived imagination, which is propelled and moved by the skill of the Evil Spirit. Thus it will be seen that it has no force whatsoever, particularly if one examines it closely and weighs the various essences of the contracting parties, the form of the contract, the manner, and the circumstances in the balance of our reason and faith. It is notorious that several deeds are attributed to Witches which these poorly-informed women have confessed came only from their imagination, corrupted by the impostor—and which anyhow did not come from the Witches but from Satan, who needs no outside help to show what he can do or to declare his actions. He is forced by no human will or power, only by God and his good ministers. This wicked deceiver obeys evil people of his own will, without being forced, although he feigns and pretends to act otherwise, as Porphyry says, for the purpose of plaguing us more by his impostures.

This imaginary pact need not be strictly binding, for it is made fraudulently and with lies by one of the parties. It could only be made through the bedazzled mind of an astonished and sleeping person, deprived of his senses. The supposition that the Devil extends his hand and bargains with the Witch is falsehood, since he is a spirit which has neither flesh nor bone. Tatian writing against the Greeks says that devils are creatures of a spiritual nature like air or elementary fire, and can only be seen by those armed with the spirit of God, but not by ordinary men with ordinary souls. Moreover, if this cheating agreement, made by fraud and chiefly invented for an evil purpose, against God's will, without witnesses and pledges, is so important and powerful that it can never be broken by any means, but that the one must necessarily follow the other's will and be compelled to obey him: then why is it that the previous compact, [when he was] truly baptized by God's special will and command and by solemn words, with guarantors and security, does not take precedence by prerogative? There is much more solidity in the contract between the true God and people of sound mind. Whatever He promises and stipulates He fulfills and does not deceive, nor does He dance and banquet while bargaining with his people, whom He neither seduces nor deprives of their senses, like Satan does with his imaginary body. If someone denies this inequality, I wonder what truth he could believe.

But you will object that the old woman has renounced the Christian faith. If we seek a way of salvation other than Jesus Christ, not observing His commandments and not following them happily with genuine faith, then we renounce his faith, and we do it with a sound mind. But in that other case, what was supposedly done by the old woman comes from the stupidity of old age, the inconstancy of her sex, fickleness, a weak mind, despair, and mental disease, when the old woman is deceived imaginarily or by the wiles of the evil spirit. Listen a bit and hearken to the words of St. Paul, where he portrays very well those people who truly renounce the Christian faith. Namely, the Spirit says that in the last days some will revolt from the faith, amusing themselves with deceitful spirits and with the devil's doctrines, teaching hypocritically, having their conscience hardened, forbidding marriage, commanding abstention from meat which God has created through grace for use by the faithful and by those who have known the truth. Know also that in the last days there will be troubled times. For men will be filled with self-love, avaricious, boastful, proud, gossipers, lacking in filial piety, ungrateful, contemptuous towards God, lacking in natural affection, slanderers, cruel, haters of the Godly, traitors, foolhardy, swollen, lovers of pleasure instead of lovers of God; having the appearance of piety and prudence, but without the things themselves. Turn away from them, for they gorge in their houses, and hold captive weak women laden with sin. They are led along by various desires, always learning yet never coming to recognize truth. As Jannes and Mambres resisted Moses, those people—corrupted in their understanding, real reprobates in matters of faith—resist truth. . . . That is what St. Paul says.

If you return to the baptismal oil which has supposedly been removed by that [diabolical] pact, this point I could answer well in a word, for it were better to answer it so that worse things may not follow. If there is some virtue in the sacrament of baptism, surely it consists no more in the external anointment than in the external washing with water, by which a person is so sanctified and confirmed through the intervention of faith, that even if he were afterwards washed a hundred times with all the water you wish and even if all his skin were stripped away, still the essence of baptism remains in him through the character which faith has left there—even if the deceived person renounces its virtue. If perchance he returns to a better life through repentance and mending his ways, the same power and virtue of baptism will remain in him just as it had formerly been imprinted there. In other words, baptism will have its same value after a person returns to the straight path. Otherwise it would follow that this virtue was abolished by a wound received on the head or by an ulcer which appeared on the spot of the anointment. Also, I think that in this [diabolic] pact the top of the head is not truly shaved, but only in imagination, just as in our opinion several other things happen in this business in order to tempt gullible and senseless people by wicked persuasion, making them believe that they are so well coated with diabolical lacquer that all exits are closed to them, or making them yield to despair and thus ready to undertake all sorts of extraordinary and evil things. But the path of conversion is no more closed to them, deceived in their corrupt fantasy, than to many others who sin grievously. For St. Peter, already warned by Jesus Christ, did not fail to deny him three times under oath, against the witness of his conscience. However, after he had confessed his fault and had wept, he was received into grace.

CHAPTER IV: THE REST OF THE PROOFS, BY WHICH IT IS SHOWN THAT THE WITCHES' COMPACT IS A FRIVOLOUS THING

Moreover, it is false, a pure supposition of Satan, and a crazy belief, to think that it is possible to make babies die with certain ceremonies. Similarly, it happens that when they claim to remove children from their graves, this is nothing but a diabolical persuasion springing from a corrupt imaginative faculty or else resulting from a deep dream. This can best be seen if we examine the graves from which they claim to have removed them, for the bodies will be found still buried. I also have no doubt that the child's thigh, put into the caldron and cooked until the flesh leaves the bone and thus made easy to drink, has entered their mind in the same way. For it is so inhuman, horrible, cruel, and hard to believe, that even if I saw it with my own eyes I would rather believe that my eyes were charmed by the spell of such a spectacle than confess to seeing this wicked and ultra-tragic thighbone, which surpasses all belief. But assume that the Witches, horrible workers with this unguent, have truly come from the bottom of hell and have cast aside any trace of human sentiment: now I ask you whence comes this virtue in this unguent, so that whoever rubs himself with it acquires wicked desires, execrable arts, and unbelievable travels? or that, after greasing a seat or piece of wood with it, whoever sits on it is immediately wafted into the air, as the Witches persuade themselves? I do not wish to argue learnedly here about the complexion, temperament and virtues of that dead flesh, rotten and venomous, for I firmly believe that they could not be found in nature if so prepared. The same holds for the preparation, imbibing, and virtues of that liquid matter in the bottle.

However, it should not be denied that these miserable little women are so crazed by the devil, through the figures which have been engraved on their fantasy, that they know these things just as well as if they had truly been done. The greater part of all their works and deeds also seems to be imaginary, so that when questioned and close to the flames they openly confess faults which they only know through dreams or apparitions. The same thing is confirmed by the Decretals. Some weak women, servants of Satan, seduced by the devil's illusions, think they can perform many other wicked acts, like tearing babies from their mothers' breasts, roasting them and eating them; or entering houses by chimneys or windows in order to torment and worry the inhabitants in various ways—which things and others like them only happen in their fantasy. Moreover, the devil plays with the Witch who makes a little trench in ground and fills it with urine or water, stirring it with her finger, and believes she is stirring up a storm; while the devil troubles the air to keep her always at her job. Thus the use of that infernal drink . . . clearly demonstrates that it proceeds from imposture, not to mention its great diversity [in contents]. Concerning this, I say with Horace that fables should not be presumed to tell the truth in everything that they reveal, nor do I think that one can draw a live baby from the belly of a Witch after her dinner.

The emptiness of this [diabolical] compact is also shown, because after making it one is forced to observe ceremonies contrary to the statutes of the Church—like fasting on Sundays, eating flesh on Fridays and Saturdays, hiding one's sins at confession, spitting on the ground when the God of the Mass is elevated, babble while Mass is being sung, or do anything else which the forgers of the *Malleus Maleficarum* have written. But any honorable man, ever so slightly versed in reading Holy Writ, will easily know how many and how great these sins are. Because Sunday is ordained to hear the Word of God, to pray to Him and serve Him, no one could look after these things better than a man who has kept his mind pure and free from the vapors gotten by eating and drinking. There are, says Jesus Christ, a kind of devils who can only be expelled through prayer and fasting. That is why St. Peter commands us to be sober and vigilant in prayer. For the devil our adversary goes here and there, like a roaring lion, seeking whom he may devour. St. Paul tells the Corinthians, "Do not defraud one another, unless by mutual consent and for a time so that you can fulfill your fasts and prayers." Thus fasting and prayer are almost always joined, and certainly by a very good command. I am amazed by what is written in Tertullian, that fasting on Sunday is a bad act. Other authors stand by the words of Jesus Christ, that it is legitimate in case of necessity to eat flesh on the days forbidden by the Roman Pope, provided that nobody is scandalized and that one neither nibbles or overeats. "Hearken and listen," says Jesus Christ, "it is not what enters the mouth that makes a man unclean, but what leaves the mouth." Similarly St. Paul to the Colossians, second chapter: "Let no man condemn you for eating or drinking, either because of a holy day or a new moon or the Sabbath, which things are shadows of those to come, but the body is in Christ." . . . The same St. Paul writes to Timothy: "The spirit says in particular that in the last days some will withdraw from the faith, amusing themselves with cheating spirits and diabolical doctrines, hypocritically teaching lies, being hardened in their consciences, forbidding marriage, commanding abstention from meat which God in his grace has created to be used by the faithful and by those who have known the truth. For every creature of God is good, and nothing is to be rejected which is made in grace; it is sanctified by the word of God and by prayer. If you tell these things to the brethren, you will be a good minister of Jesus Christ, nourished in the words of faith and good doctrine, which you have faithfully followed. Moreover, reject profane fables, like those of old women, and do pious deeds." Thus writes St. Paul, who also says to eat everything which is sold by a butcher, without asking anything for your conscience's sake, "for the earth is the Lord's and the fulness thereof."

As for the fact that, according to the pact, they are forced to hide some of their sins at confession: who can do it, I ask you, who can recite them *all* distinctly, since usually even our thoughts, our words and our acts are tainted with sin? What testimony of the divine will commands us to recount all our sins so precisely, one after the other? In what order will the publican tell them in the temple, or the brigand on the cross?

The sin in spitting on the ground while the God of the Mass is raised is exactly as great as in keeping the saliva in one's mouth. The useless words spoken at Mass merit just as great punishment as those spoken after Mass. The same goes for their heinous crime in walking on the cross. Similarly, that they enter the Church on Sundays before the holy water is consecrated, and a thousand other follies of old women, which have been promoted by devils in order to establish superstition and impiety under the pretext of religion.

Any honorable man can thus easily perceive the force of this compact. St. Augustine says it very well: all these false arts of harmful superstition, coming from a pernicious association of men and devils, such as faithless pacts and false friendship, ought to be completely rejected. And Origen in his third book on Job: Enchantments, he says, are seductions of devils, mockeries of evil spirits, mud of idolatry, brutishness of soul and scandal of heart. See the recapitulation of this work (Book 6, Chapter 25), where I again describe the nullity of these pacts and agreements.

Together with the above silliness, I will also tell what Psellus writes about the Euchetes and Gnostics, who are said to perform wicked and horrible sacrifices in order to receive the devils into all their thoughts. They assemble on the day when the saviour was crucified, in the evening, at a prearranged spot, with girls whom they know. After some sacrifices they snuff out the candles and sleep indifferently with their daughters or sisters or other women. Nine months later they return, summon the women and take their children, whom they cut all over their bodies and fill phials with their blood. They burn the bodies and mix the ashes with the blood. Then they season everyone's food and drink with this sauce, or whatever part of it they can preserve. For they think that with this sacrifice and nourishment, as something truly very evil, the divine character imprinted on us which keeps the devils at bay is completely abolished; thus the devils can approach them with more assurance. . . .

[Weyer fills two more pages of this chapter with more citations and stories, but no more arguments.]

2 FROM *Jean Bodin* *Démonomanie des Sorciers*

Bodin was one of the most talented and versatile writers of the late sixteenth century. His best-known and most popular work, the Six Books of a Commonwealth *(1576), has insured his immortality, at least in the history of political thought. But it is seldom recognized that the* Demonomania *was Bodin's second most popular work; it went through fifteen editions in four languages within 25 years (as compared with 28 editions in five languages in 30 years for the* Commonwealth*). It held the field in the 1580's and 1590's as the best recent handbook on witchcraft, before it was challenged by larger or more practical guides like Delrio or Boguet.*

Bodin's refutation of Weyer, appended to all editions of the Demonomania, *offered a thoroughgoing set of objections to Weyer's arguments. Bodin's clarity of thought and language, the range and precision of his examples, make him a formidable controversialist. His demolition of Weyer was total, extending even into his rival's own professional field of medicine, where he gave a rigorous demonstration of the falsehood of the proposition that witches were really old women suffering from melancholy: "Weyer must confess that it is a notable incongruity . . . and far too gross ignorance (but it is not ignorance) to attribute melancholic sickness to women." He also specializes in refuting Weyer from his rival's own examples, "by his very words and by his books." Bodin had honestly convinced him-self that Weyer was really a sorcerer masquerading as a physician, and as such deserved the full rigors of the law.*

When this work was finished and ready to be sent to the press, the printer to whom I had entrusted it sent me a new book, *De Lamiis* by Doctor Johann Weyer, where he maintains that War-locks and Witches should not be punished. This has delayed the publication of my book. Weyer had held this opinion for a long time; and because his opponents had not touched upon the main threads of the subject, he could have replied as though he had been victorious. This gives me a chance to answer him—not from hatred, but principally for the honor of God, against which he has armed himself, and secondly to change the opinion of some judges, whose verdicts that man brags he has changed. He glorifies himself for having won this point through his books: that Witches were now clearly and simply released, and the judges who put them to death he calls hangmen. This greatly astonished me, for such an opinion must necessarily be that of a very ignorant or else a very wicked man. Johann Weyer shows by his books that he is not ignorant, that he is even a physician. Nevertheless he teaches a thousand damnable sorceries in his books, including printing the words, invocations, figures, circles, and symbols used by the greatest Sorcerers who have ever existed in order to perform a thousand execrable misdeeds. I have not been able to read this without horror. More-over, he prints all the writers on Sorcery, the most important who have ever existed, that they may be used. What is more, at the end of his book *De Praestigiis* printed at Basel in 1578, he put the inventory of the diabolical monarchy with the names and surnames of 72 princes and 7,405,926 devils (barring mathematical errors). He counts the small ones by legions, and puts 6,666 in each legion, adding their qualities and properties, and what can be used for invoking them. Still, after having knowingly taught the diabolical recipes, he adds these words (which is mischievous). The first law

SOURCE. Jean Bodin, *Demonomanie des Sorciers,* Paris: Jean Dupuis, 1580, fols. 218r-219r, 225v-227v, 232r-235r of the "Refutation des opinions de Jean Wier."

de Variis cognit. au, #medicos, ff., says that one should not call Physician anyone who "casts spells, who invokes curses, who, using the common words of impostors, exorcises; These are not physicians." The law of God does not say that it is a mere imposture, but rather a detestable impiety. One could thus call "impostor" whoever is not content with deeds, but also teaches such wickedness in printed books, and in order to cover them up sometimes talks about God and the faith, an imposture which Satan and his subjects have always used. This is, namely, to slip in all the impieties imaginable under the cover of sacred and holy things. . . . Thus one must not stop when Weyer talks of God, since such horrible blasphemies are found in these books. Just as there is no poison so dangerous as that which is mixed with sugar or appetizing sauces, so that it is swallowed more easily and vomited with more difficulty, there is no impiety so great as that which is covered with a cloth of piety.

For Weyer agrees[1] that Witches have communication and compacts with devils, and that they do much wickedness with the Devil's aid; nevertheless, in his book *De Lamiis* he says in one place that there is no compact, and in another that one could not prove it, and in yet another that the confessions of Witches should not be believed, that they fool themselves in thinking that they do what they say they do, and that they are in the grip of a melancholic sickness. Such is the disguise which ignorant people or Sorcerers have used to let their colleagues escape and increase the kingdom of Satan. Heretofore those who have said that it was melancholia did not imagine that there were any Demons, nor perhaps that there were any angels nor any God. But Weyer confesses that God exists (as the Devils also confess it, and tremble beneath His power, as we read in Scripture). He also confesses throughout his writings that there are good and evil spirits who have dealings and compacts with men. So one must not attribute the movement of Witches, their evil deeds and strange acts, to melancholy, and much less make women melancholics. Antiquity has noticed as a strange thing that no woman ever died of melancholy nor any man of joy, but on the

---

[1] See Weyer's *De Praestigiis Daemonum*, Bk. II, chs, 4, 8, 34; Bk. IV, ch. 14; and Bk. V, ch. 9 [Bodin's note].

contrary several women died from extreme joy. Because Weyer is a physician he cannot ignore that woman's humor is directly contrary to adult melancholy from which the furor proceeds, be it from yellow-brown bile, or from melancholic juice, as physicians agree. Both of them proceed from excessive heat and dryness, as Galen says in his book *De atra bile*. Yet women are naturally cold and wet, as the same author says; all the Greeks, Latins and Arabs are agreed on this point. For this reason Galen also says that man, being of a hot and dry temperament, can fall into the melancholic sickness in a hot and dry region. Also, Olaus Magnus, Caspar Peucer, Saxo grammaticus, and Weyer himself agree with all the Inquisitors of Witches in Germany that Witches abound in the arctic region or the frozen sea, and in Germany and the Alps and Savoy. It is certain that northern peoples have as little melancholy as African people have pituity. For all northern people are white, green-eyed, blond-haired and slender, reddish-faced, joyous and chatterboxes—things totally contrary to the melancholic humor. Moreover, Hippocrates in the first book of common sicknesses and Galen in the same book hold that women are generally healthier than men, on account of the menstrual flow which preserves them from a thousand diseases. Never, says Hippocrates, do women have gout or long ulcers, adds Galen, nor epilepsies, nor apoplexy, nor frenzies, nor lethargies, nor convulsions or tremblings while they are flowing or menstruating. Although Hippocrates says that epilepsy and demonic attacks (also called sacred sickness) are natural, nevertheless he maintains that these things only happen to the pituitous and not to the bilious—which Weyer, being a physician, cannot but know. We have shown that ordinarily women rather than men are demoniacal, and that by diabolical means Witches are often transported in body and often put in an ecstatic state with the soul separate from the body and the body remaining senseless and dumb. It is even more ridiculous to say that the illness of Witches comes from melancholy, because illnesses coming from melancholy are always dangerous. Nevertheless one sees Witches who have been in the trade for forty or fifty years, from the age of twelve, like Jeanne Harvillier who was burned alive on April 29, 1578, or Maddalena de la Cruz, abbess of Córdoba in Spain, 1545, having had ordinary intercourse and copulation with the Devil which lasted forty years in one case and thirty in the other. Weyer must thus

confess that it is a notable incongruity in him as a physician, and
far too gross ignorance (but it is not ignorance) to attribute melancholic sicknesses to women, which suit them as little as do the
praiseworthy effects of a temperate melancholic humor, which
makes a man wise, serious, or contemplative (as all the ancient Philosophers and Physicians have remarked). All these qualities are as
little compatible with woman as fire is with water. . . . So abandon
the fanatical error of those who make women into melancholics.
Weyer also—seeing that his cloak of melancholy was ripped away
by demonstration and obvious truth coming from human and
divine laws, by so many stories from all the peoples of the earth,
by so many confessions partly voluntary and partly forced, by so
many judgments, convictions, condemnations and executions
made for three thousand years in every country of the world—hit
upon a much too coarse ruse to prevent Sorcerers from being put
to death in saying that the Devil seduces the Witches and makes
them believe they are doing what he does himself. In doing this he
pretends that it is really very contrary to Satan, and nevertheless
he saves the Witches; which is in plain words to mock Satan ver-
bally, but in reality to establish his grandeur and his power. For
he knows very well that magistrates have no jurisdiction nor power
of seizure upon Devils. This will not only absolve all Witches, but
also all murderers, thieves, perpetrators of incest and parricides
who are impelled by the enemy of the human race to perform their
deeds. Then he greatly praises the tariff of the Papal *camera*,
which condemns repentant Witches to pay two ducats for a pardon. In another place he says he will maintain that not only should
Witches not be punished with death by the Law of God, but also
that there is no mention of Witches in Holy Scripture, by which
he could easily be convinced. Here I call on God and His law as
witnesses, and a thousand passages of the Bible to convince this
man.[2]

To demonstrate that Satan charms the soul from the body,
leaving it senseless and apparently dead, as we have discussed in

---

[2] Bodin here cites twenty-four Scriptural passages, all from the Old Testament or Apocrypha, to refute Weyer's contention in *De Praestigiis
Daemonum*, Bk. III, ch. 35.

the chapter on ecstasy, and which is not sleep: evidence shows
that no mere soporific can prevent a man, however deeply asleep,
from feeling fire applied to his skin, and yet sorcerers feel neither
the fire nor any pain, being charmed into ecstasy, as has often
been proved by experiment and as we have shown above, inter-
preting the passage in Vergil where he tells about the witch who
promised to free his mind. Still another argument can be seen,
which cannot be answered, to show that her state comes neither
from an unguent nor from sleep, but is a true enchantment of the
soul outside the body: it is that everyone thus charmed returns a
half hour later and as soon as he wishes, which is impossible for
anyone put to sleep by simple narcotics, who sometimes remain for
a full day or two without waking up. And it has also been alleged
that those who were charmed had truly noticed things happening
a hundred leagues away, as we have previously said. But one must
also note that the composition of this unguent, which the author
of *Natural Magic* [Giovanni Battista Della Porta] has given, is not
a simple soporific, but really several dangerous poisons. . . .

    If it is thus true that the demons by a just permission of God
have the power to separate the soul from the body, why would
they not have the power to transport them corporeally? It is incom-
parably more admirable to disconnect and separate the soul from
the body and to rejoin it, than to carry off the body and the soul
together. As for me, I hold that this ecstasy or *aphairaisia* is one of
the strongest arguments, after the witness of the law of God, which
we have for the immortality of the soul, and decisive proof for
Aristotle's hypothesis that the soul is immortal if it can perform
something without the body—which the great sorcerers (who know
it by experience, like Orpheus) call the prison of the soul, and the
most illustrious magicians of that time, Empedocles and Zoroaster,
call the sepulchre, and after them Plato and Cratylus say that
soma or body is derived from *sema* or sepulchre, and Socrates calls
it the cavern of the soul. Besides these arguments and reasons, to
which Weyer has no answer, we have the authority of the greatest
personages of all antiquity, like Plutarch, who gives several mem-
orable examples of it, Plotinus, Pliny, Saint Augustine, Thomas
Aquinas, doctor Bonaventura, Durandus and all the theologians,
Sylvester Prieras, Paul Grillandus, and the five German Inquisitors
who have prosecuted an infinite number of Witches and who have

briefly written down their trials in a book [the *Malleus Malefica-rum*]. And beyond the authority of so many persons we have the ordinary experience of an infinity of trials, where the testimony, verifications, confrontations, conventions and confessions at the point of death can be seen. So it is not stubbornness on Weyer's part to maintain the contrary, but impiety, and a desire on his part to increase the kingdom of Satan.

For we have proof of Witches absent at night who have confessed the truth and the cause for their absence. We know that those newly arrived at such assemblies, calling God to their aid or simply afraid and horrified at what they saw, suddenly found themselves a hundred or fifty leagues away from their house, and took days to return from the place where Satan had transported them in a fraction of an hour. I remember recently the examples of Loches, Lyon, Le Mans, Poitiers, Chateauroux, Longny, and very many others. Just read the authors whom I have listed, who cut through all of Weyer's arguments that Witches are melancholics. For he cannot say that about those who have returned after several days; although Weyer, contradicting himself at every step, agrees that Simon the Magician, whom Nero honored with a statue, flew through the air. The ancient doctors, in great numbers, have also recorded this. It is thus extreme folly for Weyer to confess that Simon the Sorcerer flew through the air, and to maintain that the other Sorcerers deceive themselves in thinking they are transported through the air to their assemblies. Has Satan less power than he had then, which was after the death of Jesus Christ? Even Weyer says that in Germany he has seen a Sorcerer-mountebank who rose into the heavens before an audience in broad daylight, and when his wife caught hold of his legs she was carried away, and the maid clung to her mistress and was also carried away, and they remained a fairly long time like that in the air, with the audience astonished and delighted by this miracle. We read the same thing in the history of Hugh of Fleury, that a Count of Mâçon was thus raised into the air and carried away while shouting, Help me, friends!, and was never seen again, no more than Romulus, who was charmed into the air before his army. By the text of Scripture it appears that Jesus Christ was transported by Satan onto the summit of the temple, then onto the peak of a mountain. From which Thomas Aquinas draws an indubitable consequence: that Satan, with God's permission, has no less power over other men to transport them, since it is completely certain that Jesus Christ was a real man and not ghostlike. But it is enough for me to convince Weyer by his very words and by his books. He himself writes that he has seen men carried into the air by Devils[3] and that there is nothing absurd about it; and in the same place he writes something false, that a Sorcerer was sought in Germany who promised to draw the children of king Francis I from the castle of Madrid and carry them through the air from Spain into France, but that nothing was done about it from fear that he would break their necks. Moreover, he writes[4] that the Devil, disguised as a lawyer pleading a court case and hearing the other party give himself to the Devil if he [were guilty], suddenly let the bar of justice carry away the man who had perjured himself in public. He says that the story really happened in Germany. After he has given several examples of these diabolical transports, he concludes that such things are certain and that there is no absurdity there, and yet in his book *De Lamiis* he says exactly the contrary. In this one can see a light brain which gets confused on every topic. Although he rejects several historians and theologians, still he uses the Golden Legend, citing the life of St. Germain where it says that St. Germain went to see the Witches' dance and straightway afterwards went to their husbands' beds, where the women were found, as though St. Germain were swifter than Satan. Since he had transported them, Satan could have brought them back just as quickly.

As for what Weyer says, that Witches cannot by themselves make thunder or hail, I grant it to him; and just as little can they kill, or make men die, by means of wax images and words. But it cannot be denied, and Weyer agrees, that Satan can kill men, beasts and fruits unless God prevents him, and can do this by means of the sacrifices, vows and prayers of the sorcerers and by just permission of God, who takes revenge on his enemies through his enemies. Also, the Witches deserve a thousand times more tortures for having renounced God and adored Satan than if

---

[3] See *De Praestigiis Daemonum*, Bk. II, ch. 12 [Bodin's note].
[4] See *De Praestigiis Daemonum*, Bk. IV, ch. 19 [Bodin's note].

they had effectively murdered their fathers and mothers with
their own hands, and set fire to the grain. For these offences
are against men, as Samuel says; but their offence is directly
against the holy majesty of God. [They are punished] with
even more cause if God is directly offended, and men are also
killed and fruits spoiled by the Witchcraft of such people.
Hence the law of the twelve tables punishes those who have put
spells on fruit; Weyer mocks this, as he also slanders the Law of
God. But one can answer him that his vocation is to judge the
color and consistency of urine and other such things, and not to
touch holy matters nor infringe divine and human laws. For however much Weyer confesses that the agent is Satan, still he cannot
deny that Satan is incited, impelled, attracted and helped by the
Witches, and the Witches by him, to commit these wicked deeds.

3   E. W. Monter "Law, Medicine, and the Acceptance of Witchcraft, 1560–1580"

*A brief survey of the intellectual survival of witchcraft during the
whole of the sixteenth century, this essay argues that in none of the
learned professions—law, medicine, theology, or philosophy—could any
convincing "natural" explanation for witchcraft be found. Thus the
intellectual foundations of the great persecutions from 1580-1650 were
fairly solid.*

The most baffling fact about the theories of the *Malleus Maleficarum* is not their relatively late appearance, but the general degree
of acceptance they received among the educated classes of Europe
during the sixteenth and seventeenth centuries. Historians of a
rationalistic bent, from W. E. H. Lecky a century ago to Hugh
Trevor-Roper, agree that Europe produced no convincing anti-

SOURCE. E.W. Monter, "Law, Medicine, and the Acceptance of Witchcraft, 1560–1580." (Paper delivered at the Chicago Renaissance Society,
Nov. 21, 1967.)

dote to the *Malleus* before the eighteenth century. The consensus among Europe's *res publica litterarum* generally accepted
the system of witchcraft described in the *Malleus* throughout the
Renaissance and Reformation, gradually abandoning it in the second half of the seventeenth century. No successful anti-*Malleus*
was ever produced in these centuries, which immediately raises
the question, why was none produced? Or, rather, why were
those which were produced usually unconvincing?

Before attempting an answer, let us ask one more question:
why did the *Malleus*, that ripe fruit of the scholastic method, a
summa by Dominican Inquisitors of the work of other Dominican
Inquisitors, survive the first sixty years of the sixteenth century?
Considering the glee with which the Renaissance demolished
scholastic quiddities, and the violence with which the Reformation attacked the monastic orders and all their products, how
could it manage to withstand this double assault until the moment
when its validity was to be most severely tested and finally reaf-
firmed?

Renaissance humanism, which reached its peak in the decades
after the publication of the *Malleus*, did two important things
with the theory of witchcraft presented to it. First, as one might
expect, some prominent humanists displayed their wit and scholarship at the expense of this product of the old-fashioned
schools. Let us take two examples: the uncrowned humanist
prince, Erasmus, and the famous legal humanist Andrea Alciati.
Erasmus had little to say about witchcraft (which may simply
indicate that he was seldom concerned about it); his edition of the
New Testament, as Trevor-Roper has noted, was "consistently
unhelpful" to the witch-hunters at all the potentially useful passages. On the lone occasion where he treated the subject at length,
Erasmus apparently accepted the wonders performed by a French
sorcerer in 1501 as real; but at the same time, he went on to prove
that magicians' pacts with the Devil were a modern invention,
unknown to Roman law or the earliest Pontifical decretals. Erasmus introduces his story as a tragedy, not a comedy, and he closes
it with the observation that we undergo new types of punishment
today because we irritate God with new forms of evil. Thus Erasmus' critical scholarship was at work only upon the pedigree of

the magical tricks he related and not upon the reality of the tricks themselves. Alciati, a founder of legal humanism, encountered witchcraft in his first recorded case, in 1515, when he had to rule on the validity of the methods of certain Lombard Inquisitors against whom some peasants had rebelled. He began by accepting that many of the accused women were either poisoners or blasphemers who had truly worshipped the Devil and who thus deserved death. However, Alciati denied the Inquisitors' thesis that the witches were really present at the diabolical Sabbats. Buttressing his arguments with citations from Horace and Augustine, he asked, "why not believe that the Devil danced with his demons and the wives slept with their husbands? why imagine real bodies in an imaginary frolic and imaginary bodies in a real bed?"

Like Erasmus, Alciati did not go very far in attacking the system of witchcraft, although he did chip away at one important part. Some humanists, like Hutten in the *Letters of Obscure Men* (Pt I, #41), went farther and tried to kill diabolical superstitions with ridicule. But such cases were rare, and important Renaissance authors could be found on the other side of the fence, led by Giovanni Francesco Pico della Mirandola, whose dialogue *Strix* was published in 1523.

By and large, Renaissance humanism did not attack the central presuppositions of the system of witchcraft constructed by the Inquisition. This attitude was probably connected to the second major contribution of Renaissance thought to this subject, namely the separation of ignorant witchcraft from learned (and innocuous) magic.

The extent to which magic permeated the intellectual worldview of the Renaissance is well known today, thanks largely to the efforts of Eugenio Garin and Daniel Walker. Very shortly after the appearance of the *Malleus*, Marisilio Ficino began publishing his attempts to develop a reformed, Christian magic, which no longer depended upon demonic forces to produce its effects. "White" magic in a new sense—no longer the benevolent activities of superstitious peasant women mixing "good" herbs to obtain occult cures—was born, a branch of higher learning. The Renaissance magician, bearer of a higher or deeper wisdom, considered himself as the antithesis of the old-fashioned and reprehensible sorcerer. In general, Renaissance writing about this spiritual magic tried to clearly and systematically distinguish it from witchcraft, but it did not deny the reality or efficacy of black magic. Most of the daemons who inhabited the magical world of Renaissance Platonism were harmless—these are the daemons to whom Ronsard wrote his famous hymn—but this does not mean that there were no harmful daemons.

The tension between good and bad daemons, between white and black magic, was always latent and sometimes visible in the works of the great Renaissance *magi*. Probably the best illustration of this presence was the well-known and widely read *De Occulta Philosophia* of Cornelius Agrippa. Black magic kept creeping into the nooks and crannies of Agrippa's huge synthesis of occult practices, more openly and obviously than it did in such other *summas* of natural magic as G. B. della Porta's. Doubtless this is why Agrippa remained in popular imagination as the greatest sorcerer of all time (a role given to him, for example, by Jean Bodin and by Cyrano de Bergerac) and as the major source for the "do-it-yourself" handbooks of black magic, the *grimoires*. Agrippa's is the limiting case to show that Ficino's attempt to completely separate magic from witchcraft was impossible.

If the Renaissance tried harder to purify magic than to refute witchcraft, if it merely sniped at a few parts of the system of the *Malleus*, then surely the Reformation could do more. Now Papist superstitions were attacked with both religious zeal and scholarship, and was not *Malleus*-type witchcraft a recent doctrine, shaped by a corrupt Church, unknown in many essential features (as Erasmus had shown) to most early Christian writers?

But the Reformation had even less intention of uprooting the current system of witchcraft than had the Renaissance. Martin Luther, that great primitive, lived in a world governed by the Devil and the Devil's agents. Luther's world was full of black magic. The older he got, the more witchcraft he saw. Catholic scholars such as Janssen have lovingly collected his outbursts on this topic. In his early career, Luther preached to his congregation (1516) that "many people believe that witches ride on a broomstick or ram or donkey's head to some place or other where all the witches riot together as they please; but it is forbidden not only to do this, but to believe that it is done. Also it is not permitted to believe that old women are changed into cats and swarm around at night." But within a decade (1522), he was preaching that "sorcerers or witches are the Devil's whores who steal milk, raise storms, ride on goats or broomsticks, lame or maim people, torture babies in their cradles, change things into different shapes so that a human being seems to be a cow or an ox, and force people into love and immorality . . . not that the Devil is unable to do these things by himself without sorcerers, for he is lord of the world, yet he will not act without human help."

Calvin, although much less vehement than Luther, was probably no more skeptical on this subject—although he spent more time and eloquence in unmasking superstition and even wrote an excellent treatise against astrology and divination. Like Erasmus (or Zwingli, for that matter), Calvin apparently had little to say about sorcery. But what he said indicates that he did not consider witchchraft as a form of superstition. He did little to encourage, but nothing to check, a large witch-hunt in Geneva in 1545, and he was genuinely frightened by the plague-speaders who were at the root of it all. Calvin knew that Satan could create nothing except illusions and that enchantments are only lies—he despised Agrippa and the magicians—but he clearly believed in many of the evils of witchcraft.

The basic problem was that the Reformers were inherently skeptical of the Inquisitors' version of witchcraft, but they were also incapable of rejecting the core of this doctrine. Witchcraft, after all, was found in Scripture; and Scripture said unambiguously in Exodus 22:18 that "thou shalt not suffer a witch to live" (the Revised Standard Version uses "sorcerer"). Nowhere in the New Testament does the Spirit repudiate the Law on this question. So the Reformers, committed to *sola Scriptura* and soaked in it, were led to reaffirm the law of Exodus.

While witchcraft *per se* was not repudiated before 1560, there was some neglect of the *Malleus* during the Reformation. This handbook of witchcraft went through fourteen editions before 1521, but was next reprinted only in 1576 at Venice and in 1580 at Protestant Frankfurt; from 1580 to 1670, it went through four-

teen more editions. This long gap during the peak of the Protestant and Catholic reformations contrasts sharply with the book's
popularity before 1520 and after 1580. During this interval, Protestants apparently preferred to build their version of witchcraft
on something other than a monastic account; while zealous Catholics worried about the book's influence in transferring witchcraft cases from ecclesiastical to lay courts by its stress on the
civil crimes of witches (it is noteworthy that the *Malleus* was
never printed in Spain, where church courts retained cognizance
of witchcraft cases).

During this pause in the popularity of the *Malleus*, the great
debate over the reality of the whole system of witchcraft was
decided within the *res publica litterarum*. This debate reached
its peak in the late 1570's. The main protagonists adhered to different religions, professions, and philosophies; a Lutheran physician
launched the debate, a Reformed physician and an unorthodox
Catholic lawyer refuted him, while another unorthodox Catholic
philosopher claimed that both sides were arguing irrelevantly.

The first full-scale attack on the received doctrine of witchcraft was published in 1563 by a Protestant, Johann Weyer, physician to Duke William of Berg, Julich and Cleves. He translated
De praestigiis Daemonum into German in 1567, and followed
this in 1578 by another book, *De Lamiis*, which repeated most of
his principle arguments. Weyer's attack on the witchcraft system
was thorough and lengthy, the most complete refutation of the
Malleus until Balthasar Bekker's *Enchanted World* appeared in
the 1690s. Other attacks upon witchcraft, like that of the English
squire Reginald Scot in 1584, were closely based on Weyer. Weyer
was the most important protagonist to be studied by other educated men who attempted to re-establish the basic system of
witchcraft outlined in the *Malleus*.

Weyer explained the amplitude of his attack and his main
arguments in his preface:

"My object is chiefly of a theological nature, to set forth the
artfulness of Satan according to Biblical authority and to demonstrate how it can be overcome. Next, my object is philosophical,
in that I fight with natural reason against the deceptions which
proceed from Satan and the crazy imagination of the so-called

witches. My object is also medical, in that I show that illnesses which are attributed to witches come from natural causes. And finally, my object is legal, in that I speak of the punishment (other than the normal way) of sorcerers and witches."

His central point, made a few pargraphs later, was that "witches can harm no one through the most malicious will or the ugliest exorcism, but rather their imagination—inflamed by demons in a way we do not understand—and the torture of melancholy makes them suppose that they have caused all sorts of evil."

De praestigiis Daemonum is divided into six lengthy books, each illustrating an important facet of his subject. First comes a book on the history and powers of the Devil. Weyer explains that "because this whole business is connected with the impostures and deceptions of devils," this part is primarily introductory and preparatory. Book Two is about magicians, against whom Weyer is extremely severe. With the aid of the Devil and through their own malice, these men dazzle us with their tricks and deceive people through various forms of divination. They "most foully soil the divine teachings of medicine through their Satanic tricks;" some doctors and surgeons hide their charlatanism by claiming that diseases which they cannot cure must be magically caused. Weyer believes that all magicians are fools or knaves—mostly knaves who should be severely punished.

Book Three, perhaps the most important, deals with witches:

women "who because of their sex are inconstant, of dubious faith, and because of their age incapable of clear thought. They are especially vulnerable to the Devil's wiles. He insinuates himself into their imagination, awake or asleep, through a variety of ghostly forms and apparitions, moving their humors and their vital spirits to accomplish his purpose with remarkable cleverness. [Thus old women confess to crimes really done by the Devil] while their minds are wounded, troubled and disturbed by phantoms and apparitions in brains already addled by melancholy or by its vapours."

Weyer points out that these old women are very different from the learned magicians. They have no books, no occult apparatus to summon the Devil. He also argues that they are very different from the kind of poisoners "whom the Greeks called *pharmaka*" and who were justifiably condemned to death by the Mosaic law and by many other ancient codes. Above all, Weyer stresses that witches are really only old women suffering from an excess of melancholia:

"I could have collected an infinity of examples here to show how senses are affected in many ways by the melancholic humor or by its smoky vapors, which infect the seat of the mind, and from which all these fantastic monsters spring. . . . The Devil, with God's permission, can thus easily trouble the senses, stir up the humors and vapors which are useful to him, after choosing the complexion, age, sex, or other internal and external things through which new figures, conceived by the powers of imagination, are often communicated by the nerves to the optical faculty; such that many dare to swear by their very lives that they have seen or done things which never happened in nature."

Thus Weyer attempts to sketch out a complete natural explanation for the behavior of women accused of witchcraft. They suffer from their own depraved imaginations, craftily fed by the Devil. All crimes attributed to them, even those to which they confess, are imaginary—in the sense that they have not done them, but the Devil has. Weyer's witches make no pacts and attend no Sabbats; these too are deceptions of the Devil, working through their melancholic imaginations.

Book Four treats the victims of witches and witchcraft, "showing that they are tormented by devils, or possessed by them, with the occult permission of God but without any co-operation from witches or other humans." Book Five describes the cures for people thus tormented. Weyer boasts that his treatments are "totally different from those heretofore employed;" he rejects all "illicit cures" based primarily on white magic and confines his suggestions to prayer and orthodox medicine. Finally, moved to pity and anger by the punishments currently inflicted upon witches, Weyer wrote his sixth book "as a kind of accessory" to the other five. His advice is based primarily upon his sharp distinction between witches and poisoners. He agrees that the latter should undergo the full rigors of Mosaic and other laws; but the former, who are "seduced by the Devil through melancholic torments, and are not heretics" should not be punished but simply purged.

Weyer ended his book by protesting that his arguments were merely hypotheses—"I do not claim to be absolutely certain of everything I say in this book"—and predicted that he would fall into the bad graces of some learned and sensible men, especially academic philosophers and theologians, for writing it. He was correct in predicting that his book would provoke violent refutation, but he showed less foresight in predicting the direction from which it would come. Among the many rebuttals to Weyer, we will discuss only the two most important and intellectually powerful: from Thomas Erastus, professor of medicine at Heidelberg (like Weyer a famous opponent of Paracelsian medicine); and from Jean Bodin, French jurist and author. Erastus and Bodin possessed two of the keenest minds in the *res publica litterarum* in the second half of the sixteenth century. Both are best known today for their contributions to political theory, and neither has yet found a biographer capable of dealing adequately with the full range of his intellectual interests. Both men saw serious shortcomings and fallacies in Weyer's hypotheses about witchcraft.

Erastus' attack on Weyer was originally included in his thick folio of *Dialogues against Paracelsus*, published in 1572. After the reappearance of Weyer's theses in *De Lamiis*, Erastus expanded his remarks into a separate dialogue which he published in 1578. Erastus claimed at the outset of his 1578 rebuttal that his unnamed opponent (who consistently follows Weyer's arguments) has failed to answer any of the objections which he had made six years ago, and he calls upon the faculties of law and theology to confirm this judgment.

To what did Erastus object? First, he did *not* object to Weyer's demonstrations that witches cannot really perform the various deeds of wickedness commonly attributed to them; he agrees that such deeds are the work of devils and not of witches. But Erastus emphatically does not agree that it follows from this that witches are innocent and should not be punished. He denies that witches are insane or otherwise irresponsible in their dealings with the Devil; he denies that their brains have been befuddled by visions produced by melancholic vapors. On the contrary, Erastus says that witches do make a manifest pact and alliance with the Devil, and that they incite devils to perform black magic by virtue of this pact. Thus witches are not passive instruments, but in a real sense "authors and instigators" of such *maleficia*. He adds that they are worse than magicians, who at least have no overt alliance with the demons but only an occult alliance, and who falsely think they can compel the demons to do their will. In other words, witches' commerce with the Devil is not imaginary, as Weyer had asserted, and their punishment is accordingly just.

Furthermore, Erastus objects to Weyer's interpretation of Scripture and antiquity. His first reason for punishing witches is that God expressly commanded it in Exodus—and God was talking about witches, not about poisoners as Weyer gratuitously supposed. At the close of his dialogue, Erastus repeats that witches should be put to death simply for idolatry if for no other reason: "who is so impudent as to deny that sorcerers are idolaters?" he asked. Throughout his discussion, Erastus seems to be following a central line of Calvinist thought about witchcraft, namely that idolatry or Devil-worship is the truly serious crime involved here, rather than the superstitious incantations by which witches claim to harm their enemies.

In his 1578 dialogue, Erastus refutes Weyer's naturalistic explanations for witches' behavior more thoroughly than he had in 1572. As a fellow physician, he brought his own empirical evidence and common sense to bear on the problem. Obviously, Erastus says, not all witches are melancholic, just as not all are women. Although melancholic imagination is very strong and some of the witches' dreams are caused by it, nevertheless two things argue against Weyer: first, the existence of non-melancholic witches, or witches who are obviously not affected by melancholia at other times; and second, the remarkable uniformity of the visions confessed to by witches—how could they possibly imagine the *same* odd things under so many different circumstances? So Erastus once more concludes that witches' pacts and Sabbats are not imaginary.

These arguments were less thorough and probably less widely read than the refutation published two years later in Paris by

Bodin. This time Weyer was attacked by name and with consider-
ably more malice, by a master polemicist. Bodin had attempted
this sort of debate only once before, against the economic para-
doxes of Malestroit in 1568. Like Malestroit, Weyer seemed to
him basically a sophist who tried to explain away a real and concrete phenomenon (inflation in one case, witchcraft in the other)
as an illusion. Both polemics sprang naturally from Bodin's view
of reality as the congruence of ancient and modern evidence,
of authority and experience. Bodin's attitude towards witchcraft
was no intellectual aberration but an important part of a consistent
world-view. Since his mind was logical and his memory was pro-
digiously stocked, his demolition of Weyer's hypotheses merits
close attention.

Bodin attacked Weyer partly "for the honor of God" and
partly in order to reconvert any secular judges who may have
been led astray by Weyer's sophistries. Such opinions as Weyer's,
he says, must come from either ignorance or wickedness. Before
he finishes his refutation, Bodin tries to have it both ways, to show
that Weyer was both ignorant and wicked. He has two principal
arguments to prove that his opponent is wicked, two to prove him
ignorant, and finally one major point wherein he is both ignorant
and wicked.

Weyer is wicked, argues Bodin, because he patently practices
black magic himself. Citations from his books show how he
teaches "a thousand damnable sorceries, up to the point of printing the words, invocations, figures, circles and letters used by
the greatest sorcerers who ever lived, which I cannot read without
horror." Weyer has also compiled a list of the world's most important sorcerers, in order to guide the curious, and at one point he
had even dared to print "the inventory of the diabolical monarchy,
with the names and surnames of 72 princes and 7,405,926 devils."
In all these matters, Bodin pointed out, Weyer went beyond
his master, Cornelius Agrippa, who never dared print such recipes for raising devils in his book on occult philosophy. So Weyer
is not an opponent of sorcery but a teacher of sorcery, and a
singularly impudent one.

The second argument for Weyer's wickedness is his position in
the final book of De praestigiis Daemonum that witches (so long

as they had not poisoned anyone) should not be punished by secular law. As a lawyer, Bodin exploded. He angrily pointed out that Weyer did not deny the existence of diabolical *maleficia*, but merely denied that witches were responsible for them, thus placing the real criminals beyond the reach of the law. "Judges cannot bring Satan into court," said Bodin, "but they can diminish the scope of his power by removing from him the witches who help him, pray to him, pay him homage, and carry out his instructions." Weyer had also argued that repentant witches should not be punished. Bodin replied that human and divine law saw the matter differently: "when God told David that his sin was forgiven, he was nonetheless well punished." Bodin makes Weyer look like the Syndicate defense lawyer who argues that the small fry should be spared because they only followed the orders of the big fry beyond the law's grasp; or else that because they have turned state's evidence, they are no longer guilty of murder.

Boldly, Bodin accused Weyer of ignorance in the field of medicine. He specifically refutes his rival's arguments about the melancholia from which witches suffer. "Because Weyer is a physician he cannot but know that woman's humor is directly contrary to adult melancholia from which this furor comes." Furthermore, melancholics are seldom found in northern climates, whereas north Germany and the Alpine lands are amazingly full of witches, as Weyer himself knows. Thus it becomes a "notable incongruity" to attribute melancholic diseases to women.

Second, and perhaps more serious, Bodin accuses Weyer of philosophical ignorance in his treatment of the various marvels produced by devils. First, he clearly establishes that Weyer does not deny such marvels; indeed, his books teem with specific examples of them. Furthermore, Weyer does not deny the Devil's ability to make hail, or to harm, man, beast and the fruits of the earth. But, Bodin continues,

"one can say that the witches, by their prayers and abominable sacrifices are partly responsible for the calamities which we see. Even Weyer confesses, speaking about a witch from Cleves, that the persecutions of passers-by at her home, from unknown reasons, ceased as soon as she was burned. This shows sufficiently that she was the principal cause of such persecutions, because the effects ceased when the cause was removed, and the general maxim in all sciences is that the effects cease when the cause ceases."

Weyer is guilty of other forms of philosophical confusion as well. For example, Bodin ridicules his rival's definition of a witch because it explains her in terms of things which she does not do—whereas a real definition ought to "point right at" a thing and explain its essence. Elsewhere, he claims that Weyer's arguments are "all built upon a ruinous foundation, when he disputes of spirits and demons and of their actions as if they were natural things, which is to confound heaven and earth." Thus Weyer is guilty of several weaknesses: he admits effects while denying causes, he contradicts himself, he confuses the natural with the super- natural, and he cannot even define his terms properly. And on top of it all, he is an ignorant physician.

Finally, Bodin bitterly indicts Weyer as a blasphemer, a matter in which he was both ignorant and wicked. This charge stems mainly from Weyer's exegesis of Exodus 22:18 and other Scrip- tural texts, whose clear sense he obscured by claiming that only poisoners and not witches were condemned to death by Mosaic law. Bodin argues at length that Weyer has falsified Scripture and is thus guilty of the worst kind of impiety—and modern Bible translators support Bodin's contentions about the correct reading of the Hebrew text. Bodin concluded that Weyer's errors came far more from wickedness than from ignorance (he could not, for example, bring himself to believe that his opponent was really so ignorant about melancholia), and he honestly thought that Weyer was a blasphemer, sorcerer and teacher of witchcraft, and as such deserved the full rigors of the law.

While Bodin was publishing his refutation of Weyer, another French jurist, now retired for almost a decade, produced a radi- cally different approach to the whole question of witchcraft. Michel de Montaigne admitted in his *Essays* that he could offer no rational explanation for the deeds to which so many witches had confessed, but that nevertheless he did not believe them. He did not accuse his opponents of holding a false opinion, but "only a difficult and rash one, and condemn the opposite affirmation just as they do, but not so imperiously." Montaigne then relates how

"a few years ago I passed through the lands of a sovereign prince, who, as a favor to me and to beat down my incredulity, did me the kindness of showing me, in his own presence and in a private place, ten or twelve prisoners of this nature, and especially one old woman, a real witch in ugliness and deformity, long very famous in her profession. I saw both proofs and free confessions, and some barely perceptible mark or other on this wretched old woman, and I talked and asked questions as much as I wanted . . . and I am not the man to let my judgment to be throttled much by preconceptions. In the end, in all conscience, I would have pre- scribed hellebore rather than hemlock. . . .

"As for the objections and arguments which worthy men have brought against me . . . I have not felt that any are binding and do not admit of some solution more likely than their conclusions. It is true indeed that proofs and reasons founded on experience and fact I do not attempt to disentangle; moreover, they have no end to take hold of; I often cut them as Alexander did his knot. After all, it is putting a very high price on one's conjectures to roast a man alive for them."

Montaigne's skepticism was the eventual escape route used by Christendom's secular authorities in witchcraft cases: eternal doubt. Here is the real source of that "Cartesianism" which has often been given credit for destroying intelligent people's belief in witchcraft. Montaigne's position was adopted by the ruling classes of England and France in the second half of the seventeenth century, and it was also adopted in Germany during the early eighteenth century. But it is important to remember that Montaigne's influence was in the future and not in the present. This man, as he himself said, merely cut the Gordian knot of witchcraft; he did not propose a counter-explanation as Weyer had done. His skepticism is *a priori* and is not even shaken by exposure to "facts" such as the dozen confessed witches with their marks. Where Bodin (or, for that matter, Weyer) tended to believe almost everything he heard or read, Montaigne was pre-

pared not to believe what he had seen. It was a bold posture, philo-
sophically tenable but psychologically difficult to maintain.

For the basic fact about witchcraft in Europe after 1580 is its
remarkable extension. In persuading responsible secular authorities about the reality of witchcraft, Erastus and Bodin succeeded
while Weyer failed. Because no important new arguments were
produced by either side for a full century after this debate, the
defenders of the system of the *Malleus* and of the literal meaning
of Exodus had the better of the argument. One consequence of
this was an enormous increase in witchcraft trials in Western
Europe; in the vast majority of regions, the persecutions reached
their peak sometime between 1580 and 1650.

Why did the defenders of witchcraft win the debate? From
one angle, the answer is extremely simple. The bulk of ancient
and modern evidence was on their side. Witches did exist, Moses
condemned them, and so did modern rulers, partly for the same
reasons. But even more important than the evidence was the ways
in which it could be explained.

Perhaps the best way to classify possible explanations would
be through the four great faculties of Christendom's universities:
theology, philosophy, medicine, and law. At first glance this may
seem to be only one more avenue of confusion through an already
confused subject, since really thorough discussions of witchcraft
like Weyer's or Bodin's necessarily touched upon all four professions. But it will become clearer if we begin with theology and
law. Remember that the *Malleus* was constructed by scholastic
theologians and that witchcraft was accepted by Protestant theology because of Scriptural evidence. No important sixteenth-
century theologian attempted to refute witchcraft, and perhaps
the weakest single part of Weyer's argument came when he
ventured onto theological ground.

From theology, law was converted to belief in witchcraft. This
did not happen without some resistance early in the century;
Alciati's was not an isolated case, and Erasmus' doubts about the
punishment of sorcerers came from the history of civil and canon
law. In the 1530's a papal judge, Grillandus, even considered
lawyers as the most skeptical profession on this subject. But at
this point the lawyers began to change their minds. The great

breakthrough came with the articles punishing harmful witchcraft with death in the famous Imperial law code of 1532, the *Carolina*. English common law followed suit in 1541. With some exaggeration, Trevor-Roper claims that "by 1600 [lawyers] are more savage and pedantic than the clergy; the same conservative spirit which had once resisted the novelty now venerated the established doctrine." Although Montaigne was not an isolated case among French lawyers (Pierre de l'Estoile's *Journal*, for example, shows similar tendencies), nonetheless Bodin was a far more representative spokesman for the legal profession.

Thus any attempts to overthrow the system of witchcraft would have to come from either medicine or philosophy. Official philosophy, whether Aristotelian or Platonist, offered little leverage to would-be opponents of witchcraft. As we have seen, the neo-Plantonic universe swarmed with daemons who might be either good or bad. Aristotelianism seemed to bypass the question. Of course, there were some attempts like Pomponazzi's essay on Incantations which tended to undermine some of the foundations of witchcraft; but on the other hand, Cesalpino was able to construct an "Aristotelian" explanation for the reality of demons in 1580. Erastus was an orthodox Aristotelian, Bodin a Ramist. For the moment, philosophy had no clear and obvious system to erect against witchcraft. She would have one in the next century, with mechanism buttressed by Cartesian doubt, but all this lay in the future.

Only medicine was left as a profession which could do battle against witchcraft; and from medicine came the lone major sixteenth-century opponent of the system. But even this profession had its intellectual Achilles heel, at which his astute opponents struck: the "melancholic imagination," which formed the base of Weyer's attempts to shape a natural explanation for the behavior of people accused of witchcraft, was totally inapplicable to a large percentage of the accused, as both Erastus and Bodin saw. And if witches were not merely suffering from temporary insanity induced by an excess of melancholia, then they were Devil-worshippers and blasphemers whose antics would directly or indirectly cause enormous harm to man and beast.

So Bodin the lawyer, firmly supported by theology, with the

benevolent neutrality of philosophy, and profiting from a serious weakness within his opponent's own profession, routed Weyer the physician. As the lawmakers of Saxony said in 1572 while decreeing the death penalty for white (non-harmful) as well as for black witchcraft, "Weyer's reasonings are not very important, for he is a physician and not a jurist."

PART THREE

The Apex of Witchcraft Trials, 1580-1650

It is tempting to say that "if you've read one witch-trial, you've read them all." Nearly all historians of witchcraft agree that leafing through the records of these trials is the most gruesome and most monotonous part of their research. These trials do conform to certain patterns; they cluster in certain places and at certain times. We have no very reliable idea of just how many witchcraft trials there were in early modern Europe. Estimates vary all the way from ten thousand up to a million, and the likeliest grand total is probably somewhere near six figures.

The texture of these trials is more important than their numbers. Many people believe that they were pure and simple miscarriages of justice, directed by cruel, barbarous, and superstitious judges against entirely innocent victims. Famous scholars have argued that the way these judges phrased their questions, and the indiscriminate application of torture, were the only reasons why the vast majority of the accused confessed their guilt and were subsequently executed. While this does explain a large number of these trials—and especially their tendency to multiply into real "epidemics" which devastated whole villages—it does need qualification on both its main points. First, torture alone will not explain many of these confessions. England, where the common law forbade torture, had over a thousand trials and hundreds of confessions. The Spanish Inquisition used torture rather seldom (probably in fewer than a third of witchcraft cases) and required the accused to ratify his confession after torture.

Furthermore, in many parts of Europe these trials did not lead

73

automatically to the condemnation and execution of the accused. Several regions that used torture against witchcraft suspects succeeded in wringing confessions from fewer than half of those accused. This is true in both the Protestant and Catholic cantons of Switzerland, where the whole business began back in the fifteenth century and where the last witch was burned in 1782; it holds true for the Channel Islands, for parts of Hapsburg Franche-Comté in eastern France, and for Calvinist Geneva, famous for the rigors of its laws. Often enough the accused, who had saved her or his life by not confessing, was not liberated but was instead banished from the community for a shorter or longer period. And finally, it is very hard to escape the impression that a sizable percentage among those who did confess, under torture or not, really did have considerable guilt feelings; Delcambre's analysis of the large body of Lorraine evidence in the fourth selection seems to establish this point conclusively.

1 *"Judgment on the Witch Walpurga Hausmännin"*

A sadly typical case of a witchcraft victim. In one way, it is exceptional: thanks to her profession of midwife, Walpurga Hausmännin was accused of the death of more than forty children. But otherwise, it is a full gamut of the ordinary witch's maleficia. Sexual intercourse with a handsomely clothed Devil, the ensuing Devil's Mark and formal pact (made despite her illiteracy), the witches' gatherings to which she rode on her broomstick, the lethal salve given to her by the Devil, the malevolent uses of dead children and sacred objects, even the manufacture of hail "once or twice a year"—all this is a standard confession. Walpurga was a typical victim in that she was old and widowed, and she belonged to a dangerous profession.[1] Obviously, an old and inept midwife, working in an age when every sixth child died within a very few months, was particularly susceptible to charges of witchcraft.

Confessions of Walpurga Hausmännin, formerly licensed midwife at Dillingen, who, for almost thirty years, practised witchcraft and was in league with the Evil One. She was burnt at the stake at Dillingen on the 20th day of September anno Domini 1587.

The herein mentioned, malefic and miserable woman, Walpurga Hausmännin, now imprisoned and in chains, has, upon kindly questioning and also torture, following on persistent and fully justified accusations, confessed her witchcraft and admitted the following. When one-and-thirty years ago, she had become a widow, she cut corn for Hans Schlumperger, of this place, together with his former servant, Bis im Pfarrhof, by name. Him she enticed with lewd speeches and gestures and they convened that they should, on an appointed night, meet in her, Walpurga's,

[1] See Thomas R. Forbes, *The Midwife and the Witch*, New Haven, 1966, and the *Malleus Maleficarum*, Part I, question 11.
SOURCE. Reprinted by permission of G.P. Putnam's Sons from *News and Rumor In Renaissance Europe* (The Fugger Newsletters), selected and edited by George T. Mathews, pp. 137–143. Copyright 1959 by G.P. Putnam's Sons.

dwelling, there to indulge in lustful intercourse. So when Walpurga in expectation of this, sat awaiting him at night in her chamber, meditating upon evil and fleshly thoughts, it was not the said bondsman who appeared unto her, but the Evil One in the latter's guise and raiment and indulged in fornication with her. Thereupon he presented her with a piece of money, in the semblance of half a thaler, but no one could take it from her, for it was a bad coin and like lead. For this reason she had thrown it away. After the act of fornication she saw and felt the cloven foot of her whoremonger, and that his hand was not natural, but as if made of wood. She was greatly affrighted thereat and called upon the name of Jesus, whereupon the Devil left her and vanished.

On the ensuing night, the Evil Spirit visited her again in the same shape and whored with her. He made her many promises to help her in her poverty and need, wherefore she surrendered herself to him body and soul. Thereafter the Evil One inflicted upon her a scratch below the left shoulder, demanding that she should sell her soul to him with the blood that had flown therefrom. To this end he gave her a quill and, whereas she could not write, the Evil One guided her hand. She believes that nothing offensive was written, for the Evil One only swept with her hand across the paper. This script the Devil took with him and whenever she piously thought of God Almighty, or wished to go to church, the Devil reminded her of it.

Further, the above-mentioned Walpurga confesses that she oft and much rode on a pitchfork by night with her paramour, but not far, on account of her duties. At such devilish trysts she met a big man with a grey beard, who sat in a chair, like a great prince and was richly attired. That was the Great Devil to whom she had once more dedicated and promised herself body and soul. Him she worshipped and before him she knelt, and unto him she rendered other such-like honours. But she pretends not to know with what words and in which fashion she prayed. She only knows that once she heedlessly pronounced the name of Jesus. Then the above-mentioned Great Devil struck her in the face and Walpurga had to disown (which is terrible to relate) God in heaven, the Christian name and belief, the blessed Saints and the Holy Sacraments, also to renounce the heavenly hosts and the whole of Christendom. Thereupon the Great Devil baptized her afresh, naming her Höfelin, and her paramour-devil, Federlin.

At those devilish meetings, she ate, drank and fornicated with her paramour. Because she would not allow him to drag her along everywhere he had beaten her harshly and cruelly. For food she often had a good roast or an innocent child, which was also roasted, or a suckling pig, and red and white wine, but no salt.

Since her surrender to the Devil, she had seemingly oft received the Blessed Sacrament of the true Body and Blood of Jesus Christ, apparently by the mouth, but had not partaken of it, but (which once more is terrible to relate) had always taken it out of her mouth again and delivered it up to Federlin, her paramour. At their nightly gatherings she had oft with her other playfellows trodden under foot the Holy and Blessed Sacrament and the image of the Holy Cross. The said Walpurga states that during such-like frightful and loathsome blasphemies she at times truly did espy drops of blood upon the said Holy Sacrament, whereat she herself was greatly horrified.

At the command and threat of her whoremonger she had oft dishonoured the consecrated font, emptied it before her house or even destroyed the same. This she was made to do only a few days before she was cast into prison, when she was in the parish church from which she took a holy water stoup and carried it home. Then her devil paramour arrayed in handsome garments encountered her in the little street between the great cloister and the stable of Martin Müller. He desired to take the holy water stoup out of her hand and forced her to hurl it against the wall. She had also been obliged sorely to dishonour the blessed Mother of God, the Holy Virgin Mary, to spit out in front of her and say: "Shame, thou ugly hussy!" Her paramour, Federlin, came to her in many divers places in order to fornicate with her, even in the street by night and while she lay in durance. She confesses, also, that her paramour gave her a salve in a little box with which to injure people and animals, and even the precious fruit of the field.

He also compelled her to do away with and to kill young infants at birth, even before they had been taken to Holy Baptism. This she did, whenever possible. These as follows:

1 and 2. About ten years ago, she had rubbed Anna Hämännin, who dwelt not far from Durstigel, with her salve on the occasion

of her first childbirth and also otherwise damaged her so that mother and child remained together and died.

3. Dorothea, the stepdaughter of Christian Wachter, bore her first child ten years before; at its birth she made press on its little brain so that it died. The Devil had specially bidden her destroy the first-born.

4. Ten years ago she had poisoned with her salve the second child of Anna Kromt, who dwelt by the Altheim Gate, so that it died.

5. When, four years ago, the organist's wife was awaiting her confinement, she touched her naked body with her salve whereby the child promptly died and came stillborn.

6. Ten years ago she destroyed and killed at birth the girl child of the wife of the present tollman.

7. Twelve years ago she had killed at birth, with her salve and by strangulation, a girl child of the Pallingerin, who dwelt in a little house near the Danube baths.

8. Three years ago when she was called to a mill to the miller's wife there she had let the child fall into the water and drown.

9. Six years ago she was called to Eislingen to a poor woman who dwelt near the church. She killed the child by pressing on its brain at the time of delivery.

10. Eight or ten years ago she was called to Steinheim to a poor woman who lived on the other side of the river on the left bank. There also she killed the child by a special manipulation.

11. When six years ago, she partook of food with Magdalena Seilerin, called *Kammerschreiberin* (wife of the chamber scribe), she had put a salve in her drink, so that she was delivered prematurely. This child she, Walpurga, secretly buried under the doorway of the said wife of the scribe on the pretext that then she would have no other miscarriage. The same she also did with many others. When she was questioned under torture for the reasons of this burial, she admitted that it was done in order to cause disunion between two spouses. This her Devil-Paramour had taught her.

12. A child of Stoffel Schmidt she had, four years ago, put to death and after dug out of the grave.

13 and 14. She confessed that, when, eleven years earlier, the spouse of the late Chancellor, Dr. Peuter, lay a long while in

travail, she had rubbed a Devil's salve on the placenta, whereby she became so weak that she had to be given Extreme Unction. Three hours later, mother and child remained together and died.

15. She had also rubbed a salve on a beautiful son of the late Chancellor, Jacob by name: this child had lovely fair hair and she had given him a hobby-horse so that he might ride on it till he lost his senses. He died likewise.

16. Eight years ago she gave the rightfully wedded wife of Otto Vischer, when she was big with child, a drink, whereafter the child was born dead.

17, 18, 19, 20, 21, 22, 23 and 24. She did slay a child of each of the following: George Gopen, Sybilla Turnerin, the wife of Jäglein, Anna Seirin, Girg Gärtner, Klinger, the coppersmith Simon Leberwurst, the groom Hans Durst.

25. A child of the Governor here, Wilhelm Schenk von Stauffenberg, named Werner, she had so infected with her salve that he died within three days.

26 and 27. She had smeared and killed yet two other children of the Governor with her salve.

28 and 29. She had killed a boy child of both Master Niklas Brügelmaier and publican Kunz.

30. Three years ago she had sucked out the blood of publican Kunz's child, a twin, so that it died.

She confesses likewise, that the blood which she sucked from the child, she had to spit out again before the devil, as he had need of it to concoct a salve. She could work the children no harm if they were protected by holy water. But if she herself gave the child holy water, she was able to do it damage, as she had previously passed water into it.

31, 32, 33, 34, 35, 36, 37, 38, 39, 40, 41, 42 and 43. She confesses that she killed a child of each of the following: Venedigerin, Hefelinin, Landstrasslerin, Fischerin, Eva auf der Bleiche, Weberin, the wife of the town scribe, Kautzin, Mechin, Weinzieherin, Berlerin and Martin Kautzin, but two of the Berlerin.

Only a short time since she had wished to smear with a salve the small boy of Georg Klinger, but she was encountered by people and was not able to achieve this.

She also rubbed the wife of the Governor with a salve, but as she wore a neck ornament with blessed medals on it the salve did not work.

In the foregone winter at eventide she had rubbed the housewife of the town scribe on the arm with her salve, shortly after she suffered great pain and to this day suffers day and night in spite of all the remedies she has tried.

When eight years ago she was helping Michel Klingler to push a cart, and Klingler wanted to lift the shafts with his head, she touched it with her salve. Since then, Klingler is fading away and death is the only thing before him.

To the daughter of Hans Striegel, who is now in the little cloister, she gave a drink in her youth, since when she languishes and is in bad health.

She rubbed with her salve and brought about the death of Lienhart Geilen's three cows, of Bruchbauer's horse, two years ago of Max Petzel's cow, three years ago of Duri Striegel's cow, two years ago of Hans Striegel's cow, of the cow of the Governor's wife, of a cow of Frau Schötterin, and two years ago of a cow of Michel Klingler, on the village green. In short, she confesses that she destroyed a large number of cattle over and above this. A year ago she found bleached linen on the common and rubbed it with her salve, so that the pigs and geese ran over it and perished shortly thereafter. Walpurga confesses further that every year since she has sold herself to the Devil, she has on St. Leonard's Day exhumed at least one or two innocent children. With her Devil-Paramour and other play-fellows she has eaten these and used their hair and their little bones for witchcraft.

She was unable to exhume the other children she had slain at birth, although she attempted it, because they had been baptized before God.

She had used the said little bones to manufacture hail; this she was wont to do once or twice a year. Once this spring, from Siechenhausen, downwards across the fields. She likewise manufactured hail last Whitsun, and when she and others were accused of having held a witches' revel, she had actually held one near the upper gate by the garden of Peter Schmidt. At that time her play-fellows began to quarrel and struck one another, because some wanted to cause it to hail over Dillingen Meadows, others below it. At last the hail was sent over the marsh towards Weissingen, doing great damage. She admits that she would have caused still more and greater evils and damage if the Almighty had not graciously prevented and turned them away.

After all this, the Judges and Jury of the Court of this Town of Dillingen, by virtue of the Imperial and Royal Prerogative and Rights of His Right Reverence, Herr Marquard, Bishop of Augsburg, and Provost of the Cathedral, our most gracious Prince and Lord, at last unanimously gave the verdict that the aforesaid Walpurga Hausmännin be punished and dispatched from life to death by burning at the stake as being a maleficent and well-known witch and sorceress, convicted according to the context of Common Law and the Criminal Code of the Emperor Charles V and the Holy Roman Empire. All her goods and chattels and estate left after her to go to the Treasury of our Most High Prince and Lord. The aforesaid Walpurga to be led, seated on a cart, to which she is tied, to the place of her execution, and her body first to be torn five times with red-hot irons. The first time outside the town hall in the left breast and the right arm, the second time at the lower gate in the right breast, the third time at the mill brook outside the hospital gate in the left arm, the fourth time at the place of execution in the left hand. But since for nineteen years she was a licensed and pledged midwife of the city of Dillingen, yet has acted so vilely, her right hand with which she did such knavish tricks is to be cut off at the place of execution. Neither are her ashes after the burning to remain lying on the ground, but are thereafter to be carried to the nearest flowing water and thrown thereinto. Thus a venerable jury have entrusted the executioner of this city with the actual execution and all connected therewith.

2   *"The Witch-Persecution at Bamberg"*

This is in many ways an unusual trial for witchcraft. The time and place are typical enough—the episcopal city of Bamberg in Franconia during the Thirty Years' War. But the victim in this case was an extremely prominent person, the former burgomaster of the city. Very seldom did a witchcraft trial reach so highly placed a person, although perhaps a dozen cases of even more prominent victims could be cited. Second, what makes the trial of burgomaster Junius truly unique in the annals of witchcraft is his secret letter to his daughter composed during his trial, and printed here. Junius suffered horribly under torture. He was already an old man at 55, a comfortable burgher who may not have had the sheer toughness of some peasant suspects. "All this," he confessed to his daughter, "I was forced to say through fear of the torture which was threatened beyond what I had already endured."

Cases like this provide the clearest possible illustration of the abuse of torture in witchcraft trials, which was especially common in Germany. Within a few years of Junius' death, the Jesuit Friedrich Spee published his famous denunciation of judicial murder in witchcraft trials, the Cautio Criminalis.

. . . On Wednesday, June 28, 1628, was examined without torture, Johannes Junius, Burgomaster at Bamberg, on the charge of witchcraft: how and in what fashion he had fallen into that vice. Is fifty-five years old, and was born at Niederwaysich in the Wetterau. Says he is wholly innocent, knows nothing of the crime, has never in his life renounced God; says that he is wronged before God and the world, would like to hear of a single human being who has seen him at such gatherings [as the witch-sabbaths].

Confrontation of Dr. Georg Adam Haan. Tells him to his face he will stake his life on it [*er wolle darauf leben und sterben*], that he saw him, Junius, a year and a half ago at a witch-gathering in the electoral council-room, where they ate and drank. Accused denies the same wholly.

Confronted with Hopffens Elsse. Tells him likewise that he was on Haupts-moor at a witch-dance; but first the holy wafer was desecrated. Junius denies. Hereupon he was told that his accom-

SOURCE. George L. Burr, ed., "The Witch-Persecution at Bamberg," in *Translations and Reprints from the Original Sources of European History,* Vol. III, Series for 1896, University of Pennsylvania, pp. 23–28.

plices had confessed against him and was given time for thought.

On Friday, June 10, 1628, the aforesaid Junius was again without torture exhorted to confess, but again confessed nothing, whereupon, . . . since he would confess nothing, he was put to the torture, and first the

Thumb-screws were applied. Says he has never denied God his savior nor suffered himself to be otherwise baptized; will again stake his life on it; feels no pain in the thumb-screws.

Leg-screws. Will confess absolutely nothing; knows nothing about it. He has never renounced God; will never do such a thing; has never geen guilty of this vice; feels likewise no pain.

Is stripped and examined; on his right side is found a bluish mark, like a clover leaf, is thrice pricked therein, but feels no pain and no blood flows out.

Strappado. He has never renounced God; God will not forsake him; if he were such a wretch he would not let himself be so tortured; God must show some token of his innocence. He knows nothing about witchcraft. . . .

On July 5, the above named Junius is without torture, but with urgent persuasions, exhorted to confess, and at last begins and confesses:

When in the year 1624 his law-suit at Rothweil cost him some six hundred florins, he had gone out, in the month of August, into his orchard at Friedrichsbronnen; and, as he sat there in thought, there had come to him a woman like a grass-maid, who had asked him why he sat there so sorrowful; he had answered that he was not despondent, but she had led him by seductive speeches to yield him to her will. . . . And thereafter this wench had changed into the form of a goat, which bleated and said, "Now you see with whom you have had to do. You must be mine or I will forthwith break your neck." Thereupon he had been frightened, and trembled all over for fear. Then the transformed spirit had seized him by the throat and demanded that he should renounce God Almighty, whereupon Junius said, "God forbid," and thereupon the spirit vanished through the power of these words. Yet it came straightway back, brought more people with it, and persistently demanded of him that he renounce God in Heaven and all the heavenly host, by which terrible threatening he was obliged to speak this formula: "I renounce God in Heaven and his host, and will henceforward recognize the Devil as my God."

After the renunciation he was so far persuaded by those present and by the evil spirit that he suffered himself to be otherwise baptized[1] in the evil spirit's name. The Morhauptin had given him a ducat as dower-gold, which afterward became only a potsherd.

He was then named Krix. His paramour he had to call Vixen. Those present had congratulated him in Beelzebub's name and said that they were now all alike. At this baptism of his there were among others the aforesaid Christiana Morhauptin, the young Geiserlin, Paul Glaser, [and others]. After this they had dispersed.

At this time his paramour had promised to provide him with money, and from time to time to take him to other witch-gatherings.

. . . Whenever he wished to ride forth [to the witch-sabbath] a black dog had come before his bed, which said to him that he must go with him, whereupon he had seated himself upon the dog and the dog had raised himself in the Devil's name and so had fared forth.

About two years ago he was taken to the electoral council-room, at the left hand as one goes in. Above at a table were seated the Chancellor, the Burgomaster Neydekher, Dr. George Haan, [and many others]. Since his eyes were not good, he could not recognize more persons.

More time for consideration was now given him. On July 7, the aforesaid Junius was again examined, to know what further had occurred to him to confess. He confesses that about two months ago, on the day after an execution was held, he was at a witch-dance at the Black Cross, where Beelzebub had shown himself to them all and said expressly to their faces that they must all be burned together on this spot, and had ridiculed and taunted those present. . . .

Of crimes. His paramour had immediately after his seduction demanded that he should make away with his youngest son Hans Georg, and had given him for this purpose a gray powder; this,

---

[1] "Otherwise baptized" is the usual phrase for the rite, a parody of baptism, by which the Devil was believed to initiate his followers.

however, being too hard for him, he had made away with his horse, a brown, instead.

His paramour had also often spurred him on to kill his daughter, . . . and because he would not do this he had been maltreated with blows by the evil spirit.

Once at the suggestion of his paramour he had taken the holy wafer out of his mouth and given it to her. . . .

A week before his arrest as he was going to St. Martin's church the Devil met him on the way, in the form of a goat, and told him that he would soon be imprisoned, but that he should not trouble himself—he would soon set him free. Besides this, by his soul's salvation, he knew nothing further; but what he had spoken was the pure truth; on that he would stake his life. On August 6, 1628, there was read to the aforesaid Junius this his confession, which he then wholly ratified and confirmed, and was willing to stake his life upon it. And afterward he voluntarily confirmed the same before the court.

[So ended the trial of Junius, and he was accordingly burned at the stake. But it so happens that there is also preserved in Bamberg a letter, in quivering hand, secretly written by him to his daughter while in the midst of his trial (July 24, 1628):]

Many hundred thousand good-nights, dearly beloved daughter Veronica. Innocent have I come into prison, innocent have I been tortured, innocent must I die. For whoever comes into the witch prison must become a witch or be tortured until he invents something out of his head and—God pity him—bethinks him of something. I will tell you how it has gone with me. When I was the first time put to the torture, Dr. Braun, Dr. Kötzendörffer, and two strange doctors were there. Then Dr. Braun, asks me, "Kinsman, how come you here?" I answer, "Through falsehood, through misfortune." "Hear, you," he says, "you are a witch; will you confess it voluntarily? If not, we'll bring in witnesses and the executioner for you." I said "I am no witch, I have a pure conscience in the matter; if there are a thousand witnesses, I am not anxious, but I'll gladly hear the witnesses." Now the chancellor's son was set before me . . . and afterward Hoppfen Elss. She had seen me dance on Haupts-moor. . . . I answered: "I have never renounced God, and will never do it—God graciously keep me from it. I'll rather bear whatever I must." And then came also—God in highest Heaven have mercy—the executioner, and put the thumb-screws on me, both hands bound together, so that the blood ran out at the nails and everywhere, so that for four weeks I could not use my hands, as you can see from the writing. . . . Thereafter they first stripped me, bound my hands behind me, and drew me up in the torture.[2] Then I thought heaven and earth were at an end; eight times did they draw me up and let me fall again, so that I suffered terrible agony. . . .

And this happened on Friday, June 30, and with God's help I had to bear the torture. . . . When at last the executioner led me back into the prison, he said to me: "Sir, I beg you, for God's sake confess something, whether it be true or not. Invent something, for you cannot endure the torture which you will be put to; and, even if you bear it all, yet you will not escape, not even if you were an earl, but one torture will follow after another until you say you are a witch. Not before that," he said, "will they let you go, as you may see by all their trials, for one is just like another.". . .

And so I begged, since I was in wretched plight, to be given one day for thought and a priest. The priest was refused me, but the time for thought was given. Now, my dear child, see in what hazard I stood and still stand. I must say that I am a witch, though I am not,—must now renounce God, though I have never done it before. Day and night I was deeply troubled, but at last there came to me a new idea. I would not be anxious, but, since I had been given no priest with whom I could take counsel, I would myself think of something and say it. It were surely better that I just say it with mouth and words, even though I had not really done it; and afterwards I would confess it to the priest, and let those answer for it who compel me to do it. . . . And so I made my confession, as follows; but it was all a lie.

Now follows, dear child, what I confessed in order to escape

---

[2] This torture of the strappado, which was that in most common use by the courts, consisted of a rope, attached to the hands of the prisoner (bound behind his back) and carried over a pulley at the ceiling. By this he was drawn up and left hanging. To increase the pain, weights were attached to his feet or he was suddenly jerked up and let drop.

the great anguish and bitter torture, which it was impossible for me longer to bear.

[Here follows his confession, substantially as it is given in the minutes of his trial. But he adds:]

Then I had to tell what people I had seen [at the witch-sabbath]. I said that I had not recognized them. "You old rascal, I must set the executioner at you. Say—was not the Chancellor there?" So I said yes. "Who besides?" I had not recognized anybody. So he said: "Take one street after another; begin at the market, go out on one street and back on the next." I had to name several persons there. Then came the long street.[3] I knew nobody. Had to name eight persons there. Then the Zinkenwert—one person more. Then over the upper bridge to the Georgthor, on both sides. Knew nobody again. Did I know nobody in the castle—whoever it might be, I should speak without fear. And thus continuously they asked me on all the streets, though I could not and would not say more. So they gave me to the executioner, told him to strip me, shave me all over, and put me to the torture. "The rascal knows one on the market-place, is with him daily, and yet won't name him." By that they meant Dietmeyer: so I had to name him too.

Then I had to tell what crimes I had committed. I said nothing. . . "Draw the rascal up!" So I said that I was to kill my children, but I had killed a horse instead. It did not help. I had also taken a sacred wafer, and had desecrated it. When I had said this, they left me in peace.

Now, dear child, here you have all my confession, for which I must die. And they are sheer lies and made-up things, so help me God. For all this I was forced to say through fear of the torture which was threatened beyond what I had already endured. For they never leave off with the torture till one confesses something; be he never so good, he must be a witch. Nobody escapes, though he were an earl. . . .

Dear child, keep this letter secret so that people do not find it, else I shall be tortured most piteously and the jailers will be be-

[3] *"Die lange gasse"*—the street is still known by that name.

headed. So strictly is it forbidden. . . . Dear child, pay this man
a dollar. . . . I have taken several days to write this: my hands
are both lame. I am in a sad plight. . . .

Good night, for your father Johannes Junius will never see
you more. July 24, 1628.

[And on the margin of the letter he added:]

Dear child, six have confessed against me at once: the Chancellor, his son, Neudecker, Zaner, Hoffmaisters Ursel, and Hoppfen
Els—all false, through compulsion, as they have all told me, and
begged my forgiveness in God's name before they were executed.
. . . They know nothing but good of me. They were forced to
say it, just as I myself was. . . .

3   *Etienne Delcambre*
"*Witchcraft Trials in Lorraine: Psychology of the Judges*"

*The author of the next two selections on the respective behavior of
judges and suspects at witchcraft trials was an archivist in Lorraine,
where partial records of more than seven hundred such trials have
been preserved. From this rich material he assembled a three-volume
study on the* Concept of Witchcraft in the Duchy of Lorraine in the
16th and 17th Centuries. *These articles are by-products of that work.
Both of them are mildly revisionist, because they avoid the simplistic
conception that all confessions were merely mechanical consequences
of applying torture and asking leading questions to suspects.*

*The first selection emphasizes that witchcraft judges believed they
were fulfilling a genuinely Christian calling, "performing a real religious service as well as a work of public welfare." The second
discusses various aspects of the mentality of witchcraft prisoners, especially their attitudes toward torture (a test of which God alone was
the arbiter), the sincerity of their confessions (often greater than
modern rationalists have supposed), cases where the accused retracted
all or part of their confessions, and finally prisoners' denunciations of
accomplices (which were not primarily due to fear of torture). What
most impresses Delcambre, after a study of hundreds of these trials,*

is the element of sincerity and the intensity of religious feeling on the part of both judges and accused.

If the judges of witchcraft suspects in Lorraine almost invariably displayed a total lack of intelligence and critical judgment; even if, in their zeal to provoke confessions, they too often failed to meet the requirements of the most elementary honesty; even if some of them, betraying their duty, were guilty of bribery, we would be wrong to consider them collectively as monsters of hypocrisy and dishonesty, devoid of all feelings of generosity and pity. Most of them had a very high idea of their mission and believed that they were performing a real religious service, as well as a work of public welfare, in pursuing the alleged friends of the Devil. They attributed the same spiritual efficacy to the sorcerer's admission of crimes before the secular judge as to sacramental confession. A sign of contrition, so they thought, this act erased its sin. Thus one can explain the rarity of cases in Lorraine where a priest visited the condemned; if our judges did not refuse him such aid, neither did they believe it useful, considering themselves substitutes for the confessor in having saved the soul of the accused and assured his eternal salvation by provoking the admission of his faults.

Such preoccupation is shown at several points in the very form of the interrogation. They resorted to religious arguments rather than to the menace of new tortures in order to persuade the accused to talk. Their speeches often constitute homilies, recalling the exhortations of a confessor to a reticent penitent both in their themes and in their unctuous language. "We have warned her to think carefully about herself and to have nothing on her conscience, for the good and salvation of her soul," said the judges of Amance talking about a witch from Laître. The provost of Bruyères invited an accused woman from Dompierre to "gain . . . by a free and certain confession of her witchcraft . . . remission

SOURCE. Etienne Delcambre, "Les proces de sorcellerie en Lorraine: psychologie des juges," in *Revue d'histoire du droit (Tydschrift voor Rechtsgeschiedenis)* XXI, Groningen: Wolters-Noordhoff, Ltd. 1953, pp. 408–415. Reprinted by permission of the publisher.

of her sins." The judges of Blâmont encouraged a woman of Domjevin who had made a first confession to "try especially hard to recall any other deeds which she had done by this witchcraft, to declare them truly tomorrow morning, in order to discharge her poor soul of such a great and enormous sin, so that after a good confession [in justice] and full repentance for her faults, our God will be more inclined to have grace and mercy on her." In order to untie hermetically-sealed tongues and induce the accused to accept death, magistrates invoked the brevity of this life compared to eternity; those of Bruyères reproached a witch of Fontenay who persisted in denials that "he should be more careful about his salvation . . . the more so because he is today very old and advanced in years." Officers of justice presented spontaneous confession as the best assurance of divine pardon. If she consents to such a confession, a prisoner was told by the judges of Châtenois, "God will have mercy on her." Sometimes, in their length and gravity of style, these exhortations took on the appearance of real sermons. Thus the magistrates of Blâmont objected to a suspect from Domjevin who had pleaded guilty to some maleficia "that it was impossible to be a witch and to have done so little wickedness, and that, on the contrary, it is likely that she had done so much at the insistence of her [infernal] master that she is ashamed and embarrassed to confess them, and wants to hide them out of her fear of the public rather than of God; she has been sufficiently warned," they add, "how much God's great mercy, the humility, contrition and confession of a sinner and the hope of her salvation should sufficiently provoke her to search her conscience so that she hides none of her faults . . . the more so because this crime is so occult that the judge cannot judge it soundly except after a pure and simple confession by the guilty man or woman." "She would be doing much more for the salvation of her soul," they likewise told a prisoner from Reillon, "to freely confess the truth of her crime than to be tormented and to draw out forced confessions which are never so agreeable to God as voluntary ones accompanied by humility, contrition and repentance; she is not so stupid," they continue, "that she does not know very well that God the Creator knows her heart and her conscience and that He knows frankly whether she is a witch or not, and that nevertheless she should not persist in hiding her crime before God and the law, so that through punishment and persecution of her body in this world, God may have mercy on her in the other by means of a true repentance and hope of salvation." The same theme in the mouths of the *échevins* of Amance, who warned a prisoner of Salonne about her "Christian duty and the importance of her salvation and how much a voluntary confession, towards which we see that God had disposed her and was disposing her from his grace, was more meritorious, beyond any comparison whatsoever, than a forced confession extorted by the rigors of torture."

But there is a problem here: was such an attitude dictated to Lorraine judges by a real sentiment of Christian charity and an authentic apostolic urge, or must we see it as a hypocritical maneuver designed to wring from the accused, by taking advantage of her credulity and her ignorance of sacramental theology, a confession which would destroy her? Despite our prejudices as twentieth-century men, the first hypothesis seems more probable. The arguments of Lorraine magistrates, faced with a prisoner convinced of his innocence, would have been in effect stripped of all weight; they would not have had the idea of using it to extort from him any confessions which they themselves would have believed to be false. Moreover, it is important to stress that the opinion was then widespread among the lower classes that the ally of Satan who succeeded in escaping the stake by obstinate denials would not receive pardon from God for his faults. Thus, one suspect from La Vroiville having asked a neighbor "whether witches who were not executed were not damned," her interlocutor, confirming such a belief, answered "that one must thus endure the rack and do penance." More explicitly, a suspect from Pajaille d'Etival herself admitted to have "heard it said that those sorcerers and witches who die without having made a confession before justice and enduring the punishment of fire" go to hell. In thus attributing the absolving value of sacramental confession to an admission of guilt before the judges, our local magistrates, nearly all uncultured peasants, were only conforming to universally accepted prejudices. Inducing their suspects to confess themselves witches by such arguments, they thought they were fullfilling a genuine priestly function and contributing to the eternal salvation of the accused.

The good faith of Lorraine judges appears slightly more suspect whenever they brandished the spectre of hell in order to lead their suspects to denounce other sorcerers noticed at diabolical assemblies. "May she take good care to conceal nothing . . . of all the accomplices which she might have recognized at the Sabbat," the officers of Blâmont exhorted a prisoner from Domjevin, even "her closest relatives and friends . . . so that her conscience be purged and cleansed of it before God." The *échevins* of Bruyères, demanding a similar secret denunciation of a prisoner from Docelles, likewise told her that "this concerned the point of her salvation or her damnation." The theological error here seems far too great. Lorraine judges could not but know that even in sacramental confession, which they compared to a confession before secular justice, the penitent, compelled on pain of sacrilege to reveal all his faults, did not have to denounce those of his neighbor. However, do not be too severe on these judges; perhaps they saw it as a grave obligation for a Christian to denounce public malefactors (which they considered witches to be) and they judged all silence about them as an act of complicity, worthy of eternal punishment.

The violent reproaches of Lorraine magistrates towards their suspects often reflects such a spirit of piety in them and a soul so deeply priestly and mystical that simulation in this domain seems scarcely conceivable. Sometimes their language attains the highest spirituality and seems inspired by certain passages of the *Imitation of Christ*. More than once they evoked the emptiness of human esteem and the futility of the things of this world in order to induce the accused to admit their wickedness. Thus judges of the Collégiale of Saint-Dié warned a witch of Robache "that the shame of the world is nothing compared to the eternal punishments she would suffer if she died persisting in denying God her creator and redeemer." They spoke the same language to a woman of Girovilliers on trial for casting spells: "if she had the desire to . . . declare" her faults, observed the officers of Charmes to a magician of the same place, "she ought not be prevented by shame and worldly modesty . . . , all that being nothing to a person who is touched by the Holy Ghost, which imprints such charity and love of God in our hearts that we put aside everything else in order to fulfill its holy suggestions."

The violent reproach which the secular judges of the Abbey of Moyenmoutier addressed to a witch from Raon was inspired by an even higher asceticism. They admonished her "that the life of this world is only wind, worldly honor and wealth only transitory things which cannot save man without good works and without doing penance for those sins which man by his fragility commits."

Sometimes the religious themes developed by Lorraine magistrates are wholly disinterested, and, addressed to already convicted prisoners, could not possibly serve the purpose of wresting confessions from them; their sincerity thus seems beyond doubt. Some of them were simple exhortations to repentance and resignation. To a witch from Remémont who had already confessed all the maleficia charged against her, the secular judges of the Collégiale of Saint-Dié warned "that she should be assured that God has mercy on her and desires her salvation, since He has given her the grace to come and confess before justice, and that, because such is his will, she must continue in the regret which she should have from . . . offending Him, and receive death patiently, which doing she will easily obtain mercy, and that to prepare for it she must constantly pray to Him with heart and will, and for satisfaction, show Him the regret she has for her offences." The judges of Raon followed this example; they notified two people of this jurisdiction convicted of the same crime "how great and infinite is the mercy of God, who does not demand the sinner's death but his conversion, assuring moreover that God will have mercy on him for all the faults and sins he may have committed, provided that he asks pardon of Him with a good heart." Could the most pious director of conscience have used language of more elevated spirituality towards a penitent?

Men of deep faith, Lorraine judges believed in the redemptive power of prayer as much as in that of contrition. Thus, those of Amance invited a prisoner from le Bourget to "say her *Pater* with the *Ave* and *Sancta Maria*" and to "pray that God give her grace to recognize her faults and to confess how the Evil Spirit had abused her." The judicial officers of the Collégiale of Saint-Dié similarly ordered an accused man from Entre-Deux-Monts "that he say his *Confiteor* to recommend his soul to God."

Nothing in these reproaches has a comic ring or a theatrical flavor. Admittedly, Lorraine judges were rude men, inexorable and shrinking before nothing, not even the most barbarous or perfidious means, to fulfill what they believed to be their professional duty, namely the extermination of the allies of Satan. But it is undeniable that they, devout though unintelligent Christians, believed they had responsibility for souls and that in sending thousands of innocent people to the stake they were consciously fulfilling a priestly mission towards them. In condemning them to an expiatory death, they thought, from all evidence, that they were assuring their eternal salvation.

Moreover, this redoubtable apostolic zeal does not preclude any sentiment of goodness in them, and Lorraine magistrates were not always inaccessible to pity. More than once, when the accused had confessed his maleficia, they "consoled" him, although they had no great professional interest in aiding him. A witch of Saint-Dié having, after a full confession, showed her despair at the ignominious death which awaited her, "we have comforted her," her judges declared, "and warned that she must arm herself with patience; that by the recognition she has made of her faults, she is now in the grace of God" who "will have mercy on her." When an accused woman of Domjevin had recognized that she deserved the stake and had asked God's pardon for her deviltries, the *échevins* of Blâmont, "seeing her in such beautiful perseverance and good disposition and repentance, left (her) with a clergyman to console her and maintain her in such a state." All evidence indicates that an authentic sentiment of Christian charity inspired such behavior; its purpose was to soften the death of the condemned and even more to instill in him the virtue of hope, mark of his eternal salvation. It is in this spirit and "to avoid despair" which the eternal damnation of the witch would have provoked that Lorraine judges shortened the last-minute sufferings and almost always decided that after having "only felt the heat of the fire" he would be strangled before his body was consumed by the flames. This mysticism, which astonishes us in company with such ferocity, assumed a particularly naive and touching form in some Lorraine magistrates. When a witch of Reillon excused himself to his judges for the trouble which his obstinate denials had caused them, they "begged him also to pardon them and pray God for them when he would be in the other world." It would be absurd to doubt the sincerity of such language.

Those who spoke it were torturers, but all evidence indicates that only their intelligence was at fault. Their hearts were not hardened, and their love for their neighbor was not simulated. In sending the presumed allies of Satan to the torture, they believed that they were performing a duty, not only of justice and public good, but also of charity and brotherly correction.

4   *Etienne Delcambre*
"The Psychology of Lorraine Witchcraft Suspects"

Seventeenth-century Lorraine was similarly unanimous in admitting that torture, even used immoderately, constituted an infallible means for compelling witchcraft suspects to tell the whole truth without ever exaggerating it. The hypothesis that a prisoner might accuse himself of imaginary *maleficia* in order to end his torments or to avoid their renewal was never even foreseen. This barbaric procedure in witchcraft cases was not viewed in Lorraine as a normal, natural means of pressure. Applied in such cases, it was considered by the common people as a judgment from God—a seventeenth-century survival of the ordeals of the Frankish monarchy. Most men were convinced that Providence intervened to succor the innocent person and to prevent him, despite his sufferings, from succumbing through false confessions of witchcraft. To a herdsman from Rugney, suspected of being a sorcerer, who showed a desire to flee before being arrested, a neighbor advised in 1624 to let himself be taken and judged: "if he was an honorable man," he observed, "he had Our Lord as his protector, and [He] would give him every power to resist the rigors of justice." He could not have been more explicit. The prisoners themselves shared this prejudice. Several among them, convinced that they risked nothing by the

SOURCE. Etienne Delcambre, "La psychologie des inculpés lorrains de sorcellerie," in *Revue historique de droit français et étranger*, Paris: Librairie du Receul Sirey, S.A., 1954, pp. 385–389, 391–395, 399–400, 508–510, 515–517, 521–526. Reprinted by permission of the publisher.

test of torture, being pure of any pact with Hell, in no way tried to avoid it and sometimes even wished to undergo it in order to clear themselves. A woman of Bruyères, suspected of witchcraft, went to the point of tearfully telling her friends "that she wanted to be taken in order to make her innocence known." A supposed witch from Moyenmont similarly told her judges that she wished "so much to be purged of this crime in one way or another, that if they wanted to send her safe and free back to her house, she would not go, so greatly did she want to be purged." Even more naively, an inhabitant of Hurbache, indicted for the same felony, who had succeeded in escaping, surrendered himself to the law on the advice of his friends. He hoped to justify himself by the test of torture and thus to be able to recover his confiscated property.

This explains the attitude of resignation adopted by most prisoners at the provisional sentence which handed them over to the torture chamber. As soon as torture began, there was no more blasphemy, but always passionate pleas to Heaven. The immense majority of sufferers, numbed with pain, limited themselves to invoking, howling, the names of Jesus, Mary, or Saint Nicholas (patron of Lorraine), more rarely Saint Margaret or exceptionally the names of other saints. It would be tempting to see merely reflections of distress in these pious interjections; but some of the accused, slightly more loquacious, gave these outcries their real meaning. They were asking God, witness to their innocence, for the strength to undergo torture without yielding to false confessions and to emerge victoriously from what they considered an ordeal. A woman of Laître-sous-Amance thus begged "God to give her patience and the grace to endure the torments inflicted on her." There were the same exclamations, with insignificant variations, in the mouths of sufferers from Autrepierre, Domjevin, and Bussang. A more precise suspect from Amance, put to the test of the thumbscrews and persisting in denying that she was a witch, specified the kind of help which she asked of Providence: "may God give her the grace," she said, "to always tell the truth." The attitude of an accused man from Dompierre is equally significant in this regard. Having told the judges that "the rigors [of torture] would surely make him confess and accuse his own father and mother," he burst out at the moment

when his thumbs were being squeezed by the screws, "Omnip-
otent Father, lead me not into temptation" (by confessing
imaginary witchcraft). Therefore, in the eyes of many prisoners,
God alone was the arbiter of the test of torture. If they invoke
him and are pure of any crime of demonolatry, He will not remain deaf to their prayer and will give them the energy to resist
under torture. In the contrary case, He will abandon them, and
they will be forced to confess their maleficia, overwhelmed by
torture. Bearing such a prejudice in mind, one can ask whether
some suggestionable prisoners, fully convinced of their innocence at the beginning of the trial but unable to bear the test of
torture without betraying themselves and considering that as a
judgment from God, did not end . . . by persuading themselves of
their own guilt and by truly believing themselves to be witches.

Everyone saw torture as such an infallible test for recognizing
the followers of Satan that many witchcraft suspects nourished
no rancor toward the judges who submitted them to it. Even
when, after confessing their imaginary crimes, their fate was
definitely sealed and they had nothing to expect but the stake,
many of them continued to display a disconcerting deference
toward their torturers. A prisoner from Reillon, forced to admit
himself a witch by prolonged torments, humiliated himself to
the point of "praying to the judge, for the honor of God, to pardon him for the work he had caused" by his overly-long silence.
In other cases, the magistrates' stubbornness in extorting confessions from them provoked a sentiment of gratefulness which
is inconceivable to us. "She thanks us infinitely," say several
transcripts of torture sessions, "for the trouble which we are
taking about her." These sad women really had the impression
that their hangmen, in tormenting them and in forcing them to
confess their crimes of demonolatry and to do penance for them,
fulfilled a duty of charity and apostolic work on their behalf.

During their trials, Lorraine witchcraft prisoners did not often
show superhuman force of character. Only about one-tenth of
them persisted in their denials to the end and escaped the stake.
Even those who kept silent until the test of the head-clamp (tor-
tillons) and the strappado were rare. Most of them confessed
after the ladder, and a very great number even confessed their
presumed maleficia after the thumbscrews and ordinary torture.

The motive for such behavior is easy to guess. The accused correctly considered torture as more cruel than death and did not have the energy to endure the whole gamut of torments; in order to avoid them, they sold their lives cheaply. Some suspects did not hide this and straightforwardly told their judges that, having done enough to die, they preferred to confess everything rather than see torture applied or reapplied to them. Those who came around to retracting were still more explicit. Most of them justified their earlier false confessions by constraint or intimidation from torture which they had undergone or been menaced with, by care for "avoiding harder torture" or by hope for being "put in release," *i.e.*, exempted from a test and lowered "to the bottom of the ladder." Other no less material concerns sometimes explain these consciously false confessions. Some prisoners knowingly confessed from fatigue of prison and a desire to end it all sooner, or only agreed to confess under the promise of a gentler type of detention or even of a full release, which the officers of justice sometimes hypocritically dangled before them. Several testified in their retractions that only this trick had induced them to make false confessions. A prisoner from Domjevin asserted that she had only pleaded guilty to imaginary crimes of witchcraft and incest with which she was charged in order to save her son, who was reputed to be her accomplice. These temporal preoccupations may explain even the supposedly voluntary and spontaneous confessions. A fair number of prisoners did not even wait for the test of the thumbscrews and ordinary torture in order to confess their supposed maleficia, but did it "freely and artlessly" after their oral hearing (interrogation) or after their confrontation with witnesses, or even after their imprisonment. That does not prove they were sincere and were not acting from calculation. In effect, they could not have the slightest illusion about the fate which awaited them in case of denial. Also, a goodly number of them must have judged it wiser to take the initiative and immediately plead guilty in order to avoid the torments which were prepared for them. Recent examples have demonstrated the skepticism with which one should receive so-called spontaneous confessions at the tribunals of countries where, in fact if not in law, torture has not yet been abolished.

Finally, it seems certain that in a fair number of cases the confessions made to the judges during witchcraft trials were sincere. Many prisoners, under the suggestiveness of their surroundings, really believed themselves to be witches and authors of maleficia. The mental state of some of the accused explains such a psychosis. Among them may be counted women suffering from hallucinations, amnesiacs, epileptics, and even real lunatics, whose words or behavior betray a pathological state which the testimony of their surroundings confirms. Several Lorraine prisoners did not wait for their imprisonment to admit they were witches, participants at the Sabbat and objects of diabolical apparitions, or even to boast of the favors with which Satan had honored them. To be sure, mythomaniacs could invent stories of this kind out of mischief, just to make themselves interesting, but they ordinarily ended by falling into their own trap and becoming dupes of their own storytelling. Even more troubling in this respect was the case of some prisoners who, after having victoriously resisted torture, changed their minds and, sometimes on their own initiative, switched to confessions after the ordeal ended. Others would only admit themselves witches to their confessor or after a meeting with him. A prisoner from Neuveville-sous-Châtenois, after having retracted, repeated her confessions, so she said, "by advice of the priest" of her parish. Another claimed to confess herself a witch only "by a divine inspiration." An authentic religious scruple seems to have impelled these unfortunates to plead guilty. Finally, what shall we say about the numerous partial confessions revealed in these witchcraft trials? Any prisoner who had the weakness to admit that he was Satan's servant was irredeemably lost and condemned to the stake. If only the wish to escape torture had dictated such a confession, he ought to plead guilty all along the line and admit to all the witchcraft imputed to him. Such behavior exposed him to no additional risks and constituted his only way to make the test of torture stop. But a large number of Lorraine prisoners accepted only part of the accusations which weighed upon them and, in spite of torture, persisted in rejecting others. If some of them, perhaps in the fallacious hope of coaxing their judges, pleaded guilty only to the less socially detrimental crimes of black magic and disputed the most odious, claiming they were "too pitiable" to have done them, such behavior was far from general. Especially numerous were prisoners who admitted to bewitching humans, but on the contrary energetically defended themselves from casting spells on animals. One accused woman from Rosières-au-Salines went farther and took credit only for the most criminal maleficia to the exclusion of the others, having had no "wish," she said, "to put any livestock to death, but only people who were angry with her." Thus in several trials everything happened as if the accused undertook, despite torture, to limit their confessions only to those magical operations which they really believed they had done; the relative gravity of their accused crimes did not serve as their basis for discrimination.

Moreover, the sincere accents and pathetic form in which some confessions are clothed seem to exclude any hindsight or calculation and seem to manifest a profound conviction. A prisoner of Uxegney, during her interrogation, suddenly rose up "all trembling" "above her seat" and, after declaring that she wanted "to save her soul," put herself "on both knees, leaning on the table," put "her two hands on the Holy Scriptures" and cried out: "Sirs, I ask mercy of God and all of you; I am a witch."

This same awareness of guilt explains the humble deference and even the gratitude which, as we have seen, some of the accused showed towards the judges who had induced them to confess their witchcraft by their pious exhortations (plus the rigors of torture) and had thus condemned them to certain death. The language which the prisoners spoke to them sometimes reached such a high degree of spirituality and showed such mysticism that a hypothesis of dissimulation seems improbable. A prisoner from Charmes, so the magistrates of the place tell us, "thanked us for our good warnings" and swore "that at night she had prayed to God for us and that she was still praying to Him continually." A presumed witch from La Neuveville-les-Raon went farther and, after having spontaneously confessed her witchcraft, begged each of the officers of justice "to pray God for her poor soul so that it may please God to pardon her faults." Another similarly asked them "to have pity and compassion on her and to pray for her soul when it will leave her body." Such exhortations are stamped with an accent of poignant sincerity, excluding any ruse or hypocrisy.

The sentiments of repentance shown by some prisoners confirm this impression. Several among them, prostrate on their knees or kissing the earth, hands together, in tears, eyes raised towards heaven, implored divine mercy for the enormity of their crimes, prayed God to admit them to his Paradise, begged the Virgin and the saints to intercede for them with the Sovereign Judge or to help them repent. Some even gave thanks to the Lord that they were "so well unburdened in their conscience" and "delivered from the evil Enemy" by the confession which they had made of their witchcraft. The repentance of some sorcerers had a still more moving tone to it. Not satisfied with thinking of their own salvation, several of them thought while dying about the sad fate of the victims of their supposed witchcraft, and begged mercy of all those whom they thought they had harmed. "She wished," exclaimed one accused woman of Entre-Deux-Monts who had made a full confession, on the point of being condemned to the stake, "that there were no more witches or warlocks in the world, that she were the last," adding "that so long as any of them exist, it will be a great unhappiness for the poor people"; after asking for "a good confessor to prepare the salvation of her soul," she prayed "to all those whom she had offended to pardon her." Some, filled with Catholic dogma about the reversion of merits, begged "all good Christians to please pray to God for the salvation of [their] soul" or asked each of those present for "a *Pater* and an *Ave Maria*" in order that the Sovereign Judge might deign "to receive [their] poor soul when it shall leave this world."

We would not dare affirm that such an edifying attitude was always inspired by exclusively religious motives. In one case, it seems to have been at least partly dictated by a concern to soften up the judges in order to obtain a gentler death. A witch from Charmes, after asking God's pardon for her maleficia with all the external signs of profound contrition, begged the officers of justice to be spared the punishment of fire. But this unique example of a suspect and self-seeking repentance, it seems to us, does not permit one to see only simulation and bad acting in the general run of manifestations of this kind. In the last words of some repentant witchcraft suspects there is an accent of sincerity which rings true and which excludes any hypothesis of hypocrisy.

Even when they had the weakness to admit under pressure of torture that they had committed imaginary maleficia, a number of Lorraine prisoners had the courage to pull themselves together and to deny their false confessions, which invariably entailed a repetition of torture. In more than one case, confessions alternated with retractions, sometimes up to three complete cycles. If these denials ordinarily came outside the torture sessions, several people had the energy to renege during the test of the ladder, or on the point of being subjected to it. Some of these "variations" seem to have been premeditated. Did not a so-called sorcerer of Domjevin admit to a visitor in prison that if he were compelled to confess under torture, he had decided to retract everything once the test ended? The tone of these unconfessions was sometimes pathetic, or of a wholly Gallic candor. Some of the accused "falling on their knees, hands together," asked "pardon" of the judges and sometimes also "of God and the prince" for having lied in charging themselves with imaginary witchcraft. A woman from Saint-Dié said that she was already sufficiently dishonored by her false confessions of maleficia and obstinately refused to repeat them. A witch from Combrimont claimed to retract under inspiration from the Virgin, the Apostles and Saint Nicholas, and declared that she was "at present . . . much relieved." Less mystical but more expressive, a suspect from Ginfosse declared, speaking of her previous confessions, "that she had been made to say lies" and that "everything which she had [confessed] was falsehood and was from constraint." An even stranger phenomenon was that a number of the accused retracted only part of their confessions and confirmed other parts. No hope of mildness in their punishment could justify such an attitude, which thus seems to constitute a sign of sincerity.

In seventeenth-century Lorraine, a reputation for demonolatry constituted the worst possible disgrace. Several judicial documents show how far prisoners feared the dishonor of being

presumed witches and of being executed as such. Some attributed
their obstinate denials to this sentiment of shame, and there is
no reason to doubt their good faith on this point. Such ignominy
not only tarnished the reputation of the condemned but also
splattered on his whole lineage. The anguish of torture and the
spectre of the stake did not ordinarily blot out the paternal or
maternal instinct of our sufferers. Numerous Lorrainers of both
sexes, convicted of witchcraft, showed themselves haunted during their trial by thoughts of the sad fate which awaited their
children after their death. Some asked the judges' pity towards
them and begged them not to strip their children of all their
inheritance. A prisoner of Autrepierre asked the protection
of justice against the hatred which her own maleficia might
bring down on "her husband and her poor child." Several, even
more worried about the future of their descendants, turned to
the abbot of Etival (their "good lord" who as sovereign judge
benefited from confiscations pronounced against executed
witches) and begged him not to impute their crime to their
progeny since they themselves had to "bear the punishment for
it before God and the world." Consequently they urged him to
help the future orphans "with their means and to always give
[them] good advive and warnings to behave themselves well,"
confided their "poor children" to him, and beseeched him
to "serve as their father in this world." During his trial, a sorcerer from Saint-Léonard even begged "his lords [the canons
of Saint-Dié] and those who will have his property through con-
fiscation to be guardians for [the seven orphans he would be leaving and to] distribute some part of his goods to them, for God
and as alms." A prisoner from Entre-Deux-Monts admitted to
having first denied his witchcraft solely in order to avoid the
seizure of his goods, which would strip his son of his entire patri-
mony. Inversely, a woman from Girovilliers, stubbornly denying the maleficia charged to her, pointed out to her judges, in
order to justify her good faith, that if she were a witch she
would have no interest in hiding the fact, because she had no
children. . . .

What many prisoners sought most of all was to save the honor
of their lineage, a very strong sentiment in an age when family
solidarity was no empty word. Their greatest fear was that their

children would be reputed witches' sons because of the parental confession. Despite the worst of tortures, that preconception made more than one father hesitate before confessing himself a sorcerer.

Unfortunately, many prisoners, far from opposing judicial pressure to make them talk, denounced supposed accomplices obligingly and often with a zeal which makes one shudder when one thinks of the tragic consequences which such intemperance of language caused. Not satisfied with compromising one or two people, which it seems would have sufficed to exempt them from torture, several suspects listed eight, ten, sixteen, and up to nineteen names of witches and warlocks whom they claimed to have seen at the Sabbat. Numerous condemned women, confronted at the site of their execution with the victims of their denunciations, persisted in their accusations even while they awaited death, fixed to the stake with a rope around their necks to strangle them, and with the fire already lit. To reinforce the weight of their accusations, some boldly affirmed that they would not dare compromise their eternal salvation by false accusations while at the point of appearing before their Sovereign Judge, and that they therefore deserved total credence. More than once the tribunal or the site of the execution were the theater for atrocious scenes. Under suspicion because of already-condemned witches, men or women fell on their knees, in tears, hands together, begging them to "think better in [their] conscience" or prayed God to give their accuser the grace to tell the truth. Far from wavering because of such reproaches, the condemned hardened their attitude, "turned their head to the other side without" deigning to answer, or declared they did not want to damn themselves through a retraction made from courtesy. Warned not to accuse the innocent under penalty of damnation, several of the executed, "being at the said stake before many people," nonetheless persisted up to the final moment in charging their supposed accomplices and died in these sinister dispositions. On the point of perishing, one of them, "her hands together" and with all the marks of profound piety, accused two co-participants at the Sabbat. Confronted with one of the unfortunates at the foot of the stake, she stared at her and claimed to recognize her perfectly well.

A still more tragic circumstance was that the victims of these homicidal denunciations were not always strangers. Very many witchcraft prisoners cast suspicion upon their nearest relatives, trampling all family sentiment underfoot. If denunciations of brothers or sisters, uncles or aunts, brothers or sisters-in-law were relatively rare, other cases of wives accusing husbands and vice versa, mothers-in-law accusing daughters-in-law, and children accusing their mother or father of taking them to the Sabbat were more numerous. By an even less natural act, parents accused of witchcraft fairly often charged their sons or daughters with the same crime. But the most fearsome in this domain were children below the age of puberty. With a real frenzy of denuncations, a young witch of Brouaumont aged nine went to the point of accusing every member of her family —father, mother, grandparents, uncles and aunts—then induced her father to confirm her remarks and led all her relatives to the stake. One adult followed her example and, among her nineteen supposed accomplices at the Sabbat, cited her husband, her daughter and her sister. . . .

Hallucinations and the fear of torture will not explain all the false accusations which too many Lorraine suspects, sometimes with frankly hostile insistence, made about others. If no individual, no matter how upright, was immune for persecution for witchcraft in the seventeenth century, immorality nevertheless constituted an unfavorable prejudice in this domain. A fairly large number of those accused of such crimes were people of ill reputation and slight desirability: thieves, swindlers, fornicators, incestuous, sexual perverts, rapists, procurers, people without religion and blasphemers, poisoners, and above all quarrelsome or bad-tempered persons, those "inclined to an extreme anger," furnished an appreciable contingent to the tribe of reputed witches. Among these suspects of dubious honor, the thirst for vengeance was often stronger than the fear of hell. Even at the moment of death, more than one of them did not hesitate to attempt to destroy his enemies by calumny. Some of

them only did so at the "persuasion" of third parties, but most
of them had no need of external impulses to commit this criminal
infamy.

It has been established that hate played a considerable role in
the cascades of denunciations which characterized some Lorraine witchcraft trials. Numerous suspects, retrating their first
accusations, admitted that they made them "evilly and falsely,"
"from envy and anger" or "from hatred and vindictiveness."
In more than one case, such a sentiment is easy to explain. Many
prisoners on trial for witchcraft denounced as their accomplices
not random people, but those who . . . had called them witches,
indicted them as such before the law, or else had played the
role of prosecution witnesses. While retracting, many admitted
having deliberately made such a choice of people. The victims of
these maneuvers were not deceived. A defendant from Domjevin accused a previously-executed witch of having mentioned
her from hatred of her for testifying against him. Two other
defendants treated their denouncers as "whores." Perhaps in thus
revenging themselves upon their accusers, people on trial hoped
to lead them to a more repentant frame of mind and compel
them to repudiate their testimony for the prosecution. Placed in
a case of self-defence, they would be happy to turn the poisoned
weapons pointed against them back on their enemies. Can they
be blamed for it? The generalisation of such a practice would at
least have offered the advantage of making false witnesses to
witchcraft less bold and less sure of impunity. A defendant
from Lamarche, in Barrois, on trial for witchcraft, showed
himself more clever and had a marvelous idea. On the point
of condemnation, he began to accuse not those who had denounced him but all his judges, from the prosecutor of Bassigny
down to the clerk. "The case seemed so embarrassing," says
Dumont in relating this fact, "that they went twice to Langres
on orders to discuss it with the most famous lawyers of that
city." It is regrettable that accused witches in Lorraine never,
at least to our knowledge, conceived such a stratagem. If such
had been the case, fewer stakes would have been lit in Lorraine,
and Nicolas Remy (chief prosecutor of the Duchy) would doubtless have showed a little less zeal in pursuing the Devil's
friends.

But some more odious accusations did not even have the excuse of self-defense. A woman thus denounced as her accomplice at the Sabbat a woman from Uxegney whose sole wrong was to have incited her son-in-law to beat her and curse her. Another defendant accused a resident of Saint-Dié whose son-in-law, while distributing alms to the poor, refused to give her bread. Finally, several of the accused, repudiating their false testimony and attributing it to vengeance, did not specify their motives. . . . In this domain, still more horrible were the denunciations aroused by the prisoners' family hatreds. For instance, a woman from Brouaumont denounced her youngest son from dislike for her daughter-in-law, who moreover felt the same way about her. The unhappy man vainly and tearfully upbraided his mother for wishing to make him die, but she persisted in her allegations. A grandson of this unnatural grandmother aged eleven similarly reproached her for hating him and trying to destroy him because he had called her "*genaxe*," or witch. From horror of his whole family and particularly his mother, the youngest son of this same shrew finally denounced his whole clan, except for his wife and one brother. Some conjugal dramas which we have cited, during which the spouses poured the most violent and acrimonious abuse on each other, similarly prove that their mutual accusations of witchcraft were not inspired solely by a care to tell the truth in order to "discharge their soul" and to assure a repentant and absolving death for their marriage partners. We know, for instance, that a husband accused by a witch of Fomerey beat her and sometimes drove her from the house; and that a woman from Bruyères, accused of witchcraft by her imprisoned husband, . . . "had an evil head" and "was very terrible" towards him. Quarrels were frequent in this unhappy household, to the point where the husband had thought of fleeing to Germany in order to avoid sleeping with his redoubtable companion. Even some parricidal denunciations were inspired by rancor or by sordid private concerns. For example, a son threatened to have his mother burned as a witch in order to appropriate a piece of property which they were disputing. These abominable although isolated facts seem revealing for sociological history, and apparently confirm that family customs in seventeenth-century Lorraine were marked by extreme coarseness. Of course, bad households can be found in all times and all latitudes, and hateful rivalries between mother-in-law and daughter-in-law are not particular to any civilization; but the relentlessness shown by so many Lorraine prisoners in pursuing their closest relatives with calumnious hatred and homicide seems to indicate how far from tender were our rural households at that time.

Superhuman firmness in some of the accused who kept silent despite torture, and extravagant loquacity in others who confessed their deeds of witchcraft and gave the names of their accomplices—these are the two authentic traits which characterize the attitude of witchcraft suspects facing their judges in Lorraine. There is an easy way, springing spontaneously to mind, to explain this double behavior, which was not confined to ducal Lorraine: the instinct of self-preservation and the fear of death could justify the first, and terror of torture could explain the second. We have no idea of disputing the basic foundation of such a thesis, which evidently contains a very large part of the truth, but which will not explain all the phenomena. In effect, the anguish of torture is always more cruel than death. As recent experience has shown, few defendants, when undergoing such tests, persist in denials to save their lives, unless imperious reasons of a higher order push them to heroic resistance. Moreover, the fear of torture does not explain why many Lorraine witchcraft suspects admitted to only partial confessions which did not protect them from torture, nor why others, on the contrary, handed to the justices more names of supposed accomplices than were necessary to put an end to their sufferings. Beyond the double fear which we have mentioned, there are two psychological factors upon which, in our opinion, historians of witchcraft have not sufficiently insisted in their description of the state of the accused's soul. First, it has been established that a more important number of witchcraft suspects than we like to think, prompted by their social milieu or by the peremptory tones of their judges, truly believed themselves to be witches, perpetrators of maleficia and participants at the Sabbat. Some had been victims of such hallucinations even before being arrested; others became so in the course of their trial. In denouncing themselves, as well as their presumed accomplices, they believed that they were obeying the commands of their conscience, that they deserved divine pardon by the sincerity of their confession, and that they opened the path to heaven to the other participants in the Sabbat whom they revealed to the judges.

In effect, and we should here insist on the second factor, the faith of our ancestors was more spontaneous and more alive than that of even our devout contemporaries. For them, the world beyond was no metaphysical concept, but a concrete reality whose idea recurred constantly in their lives and obsessed their last moments. Their supreme goal was not to avoid death by the artifice of a denial . . . but to escape the eternal damnation which was promised to perjurors. For the better-balanced defendants who kept wholly conscious of their innocence to the end, the problem remained of the same type although reversed: better, they thought, to undergo an atrocious but fleeting torture than to run the risk of hell in admitting imaginary witchcraft and in thus violating their oath before God to tell the truth.

PART FOUR

The Decline of Witchcraft, 1650-1700

Students of European history have long known that the persecution of witches was declining in the second half of the seventeenth century, but this phenomenon has been little studied. Of course, we should note at the outset that the rhythm of persecutions was not the same everywhere. Certain regions (Sweden, Austria, New England, and others) reached their statistical peaks in this period, and a few places (like Poland) actually reached their zenith of persecution only in the early eighteenth century. But generally, Europe saw her last serious outbreak of witch-trials during the later 1600's. Perhaps more important is the fact that the cultural leaders of seventeenth-century Europe— the English, French, and Dutch—were definitively abandoning the persecution of witches after 1650. Many smaller governments slavishly followed the styles of Versailles or London in this as in so many other matters; this is clearly the case for the border regions between France and Germany.

However, the end of persecution in the principal European nations was not, as we would like to believe, a direct consequence of the enormous scientific advancement of the seventeenth century, from Galileo and Descartes to Leibniz and Newton. This point was recently and brilliantly made by Hugh Trevor-Roper:[1]

"The decline and apparently final collapse of the witch-craze in the late 17th century, while other such social stereotypes retained their

[1] Trevor-Roper, *Religion the Reformation, and Social Change,* pp. 168–69.

III

power, is a revolution which is surprisingly difficult to document. We see the controversies continue . . . And yet on neither side are the arguments new; they are the arguments which have always been used . . . Nevertheless, without new argument on either side, the intellectual belief quietly dissolved."

The solution to this paradox is to be sought not in the writings of the "experts" on witchcraft in the seventeenth century, nor in the writings of the great scientists themselves, but in a subtle change of weltanschaung among Europe's ruling classes:[2]

"What ultimately destroyed the witch-craze on an intellectual level was not the two-edged arguments of the skeptics, nor was it modern 'rationalism,' which could exist only within a new context of thought. It was not even the arguments of Bekker, tied as they were to Biblical fundamentalism. It was the new philosophy, a philosophical revolution which changed the whole concept of Nature and its operations."

The only other recent historian to tackle this problem in detail, Robert Mandrou, has also complained (in selection three) about this lack of precise documentation and has also stressed that mere "progress of enlightenment" or of Cartesianism is insufficient to explain this change. In many ways, seventeenth-century objections to witchcraft had not gone so very far beyond Weyer's or Montaigne's arguments, but their arguments were now accepted. Why?

The selections in this section are all taken from France. My justification for so doing is that France was the single most influential country in Europe in the second half of the seventeenth century; that she produced some of the most eloquent "libertines" (Cyrano de Bergerac) and some of the very best philosophers (Malebranche) who wrote about witchcraft; and finally that only for France do we possess a detailed study of the rejection of witchcraft by a present-day historian (Mandrou).

[2] *Ibid.*, p. 180.

1

Cyrano de Bergerac
A Letter Against Witches" (1654)

The archetypical "libertine" and skeptic, model for the famous nine-teenth-century theatrical figure with the long nose, Cyrano was a prolific essayist. His writings are remarkable less for their originality (like most libertines of his age, he had very little of this) than for the vigor of his prose. His ideas about witchcraft, in fact, are almost exclusively taken from Montaigne.[1] But his procedure is radically different from Montaigne's; Cyrano is more concerned to kill witchcraft by ridicule and thus less detached in his tone than Montaigne. And attempting to ridicule belief in witchcraft was a novel and daring approach in the 1650's.

The reader should notice two things in Cyrano's argument that truly show the "libertine" temper at work. The first is his care to preserve at least the appearance of Christian orthodoxy. The second is Cyrano's undisguised class contempt for the rustic peasantry among whom witchcraft proliferated; phrases like "the brainless caprices of an ignorant villager," "the crack-brained head of a ridiculous shepherd," "this old clod of a shepherd," spring naturally to his pen and are near the very center of his ridicule.

Consider how many Witches throughout the world have been convicted of making a pact with the devil and have been burned, and how many wretched people have admitted at the stake that they had attended the Sabbat. Some of them, under questioning, have even confessed to the judges that at their feasts they had eaten children who, after the death of the condemned person, have been found fully alive and who understood nothing

[1] Compare above, p. 67f.

SOURCE. Cyrano de Bergerac, "Lettre contre les sorciers" (1654) translated from Frederic Lachevre, ed., *Les Oeuvres Libertines de Cyrano de Bergerac*, Vol. II, Paris: Librairie Honore Champion, 1912, pp. 211–218. Reprinted by permission of the publisher.

when the subject was mentioned to them. One ought not believe everything about a man, because a man can say anything. Even if, by God's special permission, a soul can return to earth to ask someone for the help of his prayers, should one believe that Spirits or Intelligences (if there be any) are so playful as to oblige the brainless caprices of an ignorant villager? that they appear at either end of a field, depending on whether the black humour is stronger or weaker in the crack-brained head of a ridiculous Shepherd? that they rise to the bait like a falcon on the Hunter's wrist and, according to this rascal's whim, dance the *guimbarde* or the *matassins?* No, I do not believe in Witches, even though several important people do not agree with me; and I defer to no man's authority, unless it is accompanied by reason or comes from God, who alone should be believed about what He says simply because He says it. Neither the name of Aristotle, more learned than I, nor that of Plato, nor that of Socrates will persuade me, unless my judgment is convinced by reason of what they say. . . . Reason alone is my ruler, to whom I voluntarily pay homage. Besides, I know from experience that the most sublime minds have made the worst blunders; since they fall from greater heights, they fall farther. Finally, our fathers were often mistaken in the past, their nephews are mistaken today, and ours will be mistaken some future day.

So do not embrace an opinion because many people hold it, or because it is the thought of some great Philosopher, but only because we see more likelihood that it be true than false. For my part, I make fun of Pedants who have no stronger arguments to prove what they say than to allege that it is a maxim, as if their maxims were much more certain than their other propositions. I will believe them, however, if they show me a Philosophy whose principles cannot be doubted, which agrees with all of Nature, or which has been revealed to us from on high. Otherwise I make fun of it, for it is easy to prove anything you want when principles are adjusted to opinions, and not opinions to principles. Beyond that, if it were just to defer to the opinions of these great men, and if I were forced to admit that the first Philosophers have established these principles, I would surely force them to admit in their turn that the Ancients, like us, did not always write what they believed. Often the Laws and Religion of their country compelled them to accommodate their precepts to political interests and needs. That is why one ought to believe about a man only what is human, i.e., possible and ordinary. Therefore I admit no Witches until someone proves it to me.

If someone can demonstrate it to me by stronger and more pressing arguments than my own, I will undoubtedly tell him, "Welcome, sir; I have been waiting for you, I renounce my opinions and I embrace yours!" Otherwise, what advantage would the clever man have over the fool, if he thought what the fool thinks? People should be satisfied when a great soul pretends to acquiesce in the sentiments of the greatest number, not resisting the torrent, without trying to put handcuffs on his reason. On the contrary, a Philosopher ought to judge the crowd, and not judge like the crowd. However, I am not so unreasonable that, after escaping from the tyranny of authority, I wish to establish my own without proof. Therefore you will approve that I tell you my motives for doubting so many strange effects which are told about the Spirits. It seems to me that I have observed many important things in order to get free of that chimera.

First, I have almost never been told a story about Witches that did not ordinarily take place three or four hundred leagues away. This remoteness made me suspect that they wanted to deprive the listener of the desire and power to learn about it himself. In addition, this band of men dressed as cats is located in the middle of the countryside, without witnesses. The Faith of one person alone should be suspect in such a miraculous thing. Close to a village, it is easier to deceive idiots. The woman was poor and old. She was poor: necessity might have constrained her to lie for money. She was old: age had weakened her reason. Age makes one gossipy: she invented this story to amuse her neighbors. Age weakens the sight: she mistook a Hare for a Cat. Age makes one afraid: she thought she saw fifty instead of one. Because finally it is more likely that something happened which is seen every day and not a supernatural adventure, without logic or precedent.

But, if you please, examine one of these captured Witches. You will find that he is a very crass Peasant, whose mind is in-

capable of disentangling the mesh which holds him. His understanding has been deadened by the greatness of his peril, so that
his soul is not active enough to let him justify himself. He
would not even dare to reply pertinently, for fear of having the
preoccupied [judges] believe that the Devil is speaking through
his mouth. If however he says not a word, everybody cries that
he is convicted in his conscience, and immediately he is
thrown into the fire. But is the Devil, who could formerly change
him into a cat, so foolish not to change him now into a fly, so
that he can fly away? The Witches (they say) have no power
after they are in the hands of the law. Oh! by my faith! that is
well invented. Thus Master Jean Guillot, whose father stole the
property of his ward, acquired through the twenty thousand
pilfered crowns which his Office of Judge cost him, the power
to command Devils; truly, Devils have great respect for Thieves.
But these Devils should at least remove this poor unhappy
man, their very humble servant, when they knew that a campaign was underway to seize him: for to abandon their followers in this way discourages anyone from serving them . . .

I have also noticed that all these presumed Magicians are
beggars like Diogenes. O Heaven! is it so likely that a man
would expose himself to eternal fires, with the hope of remaining
poor, hated, hungry, and in continual fear of being grilled on
the public square? Satan should give him, not oak leaves, but
heavy [Spanish] *pistoles* to buy Offices which would put him on
the right side of the Law. But you will see that the Demons of
these times are extremely stupid, and that they lack the wit to
imagine such finesses. This old clod of a Shepherd whom you
hold in your prisons, a day away from being boiled, on what
convictions do you condemn him? He was surprised while reading the Wolf's *paternoster*. Ha! please have him repeat it. You
will find only great silliness there, and less evil than there is in a
kill-devil [an amulet worn for protection from devils], for which
however no one is put to death. Beyond that, it is said that he
bewitched flocks. Either he did it by words or by the secret
properties of some natural poisons. By words? I don't believe
that the twenty-four letters of the alphabet hold, in their gram-
mar, the occult malignity of such a real venom, nor that to
open one's mouth, grit one's teeth and put one's tongue on

one's palate in such-and-such a way has the power to sicken sheep or to cure them. If you answer me that it happens because of the pact, [I reply that] I have not yet found in my chronology the time when the devil agreed with mankind that, when one articulated certain words specified in the contract, [the devil] would kill; with others, he would cure; and that with others, he would come to talk with us. I wish that he had passed this contract with a private person: that person would not have everyone's consent to oblige us to that agreement. When some dullard, without thinking, speaks certain syllables, the devil flies straight there to frighten him and would not give the slightest visit to a powerful, depraved, illustrious, witty person who gave himself to him with all his heart and who, by his example, would cause the loss of a hundred thousand souls.

Perhaps you will admit to me that magic words have no power, but that wizards hide under barbaric words the malign properties of the simple things with which they poison livestock? Well then, why not make them die as poisoners and not as sorcerers? They confess (you reply) to attending the Sabbat, to sending Devils into the bodies of some people who, in effect, are demoniacal. As for the trips to the Sabbats, here is my belief: with the soporific drugs with which they anoint themselves while awake, they imagine that they are soon transported, straddling a broomstrick, through the chimney into a room where one can revel, dance, make love, or kiss the ass of a goat. The strong imagination of these Phantoms shows them, in sleep, little things like a broomstick between their legs, a countryside over which they pass in flight, a goat, a feast, and other Ladies. So when they wake up, they think they have seen what they have just dreamed.

As for demonic possession, I will also give you my thoughts with the same frankness. In the first place, I find that one encounters ten thousand women for every man there. Is the Devil so ribald as to seek the embraces of women so arduously? No, no, but I guess the cause—a woman has a ligher mind than a man and is consequently bolder in inventing comedies of this kind. She hopes that a little Latin which she garbles, a few grimaces, a few leaps, acrobatics and postures, will always be believed to be very far beyond the strength and modesty of a girl.

And finally she thinks herself so strong in her weakness that, once the imposture is discovered, her extravagances will be attributed to some suffocation of the womb, or that at worst it will be pardoned on account of the infirmity of her sex. You will perhaps answer that even if there are cheats among them, nothing is proved against those who are truly possessed. But if that is your Gordian knot, I will soon be your Alexander.

Let us examine, without care for shocking popular opinion, whether there were demoniacs in times past and whether there are any today. I do not doubt that some formerly existed, because the sacred Books assure us that a Chaldean woman, by magic arts, sent a Demon into the corpse of the Prophet Samuel and made it speak; that David conjured with his harp the one by which Saul was obsessed; and that our Saviour Jesus Christ expelled Devils from the bodies of some Hebrews and sent them into the bodies of pigs. But we are obliged to believe that the Devil's Empire ceased when God came into the world; that the Oracles were snuffed out under the Messiah's cradle, and that Satan forever lost his power of speech at Bethlehem, the changed influence of the Star of the three Kings having doubtless given him a disease of the tongue.

Therefore I laugh at all the present-day possessed and will continue to laugh at them until the Church commands me to believe them. To imagine that Gaufridi's parishioner, or that nun from Loudun, or that girl from Evreux were bedevilled because they turned somersaults, made grimaces and gambols! Scaramouche, Colle and Cardelino will easily outdo them. How then! they cannot even speak Latin? Lucifer takes poor care of his Devils in not sending them to secondary school. Some of them respond correctly enough when the Exorcist recites a prayer from the Breviary, which they scramble through somehow by the force of repetition. Barring that, you see them imitate madmen and pretend a perpetual mental distraction to everything preached at them. However, I surprised some of them attentively enjoying in passing some verse from their Office in order to answer appropriately, like those who wish to sing at Vespers and don't know the part, waiting in their hiding place for the "Gloria Patri, etc." to bawl it out.

I also find highly diverting their hesitations when they are embarrassed whether they must obey or not obey. The Conjuror commands one of them to kiss the ground every time he speaks the holy name of God! This Devil of obedience did it very devoutly; but when their came another test ordering her to do the same thing in terms to which she was not accustomed (for he commanded her by the Co-eternal son of the Sovereign Being), this demoniacal novice, who was no Theologian, lay flat, blushed, and broke into insults, until the Exorcist quieted her down by more ordinary words. . . . Moreover, I noticed that when the Priest raised his voice, the Devil raised his anger, often at words of no importance, because he had pronounced them with more vividness. On the contrary, he swallowed exorcisms to make one tremble sweetly as milk, because the Exorcist, tired from shouting, had pronounced them in a low voice. But it was far worse when, some time afterwards, an Abbot conjured them. They were not made for his style, and therefore those who wanted to respond answered so incorrectly that all those poor Devils on whose forehead some modesty still remained became ashamed. Afterwards, the whole day through, it was impossible to draw an evil word from their mouth. In truth, they cried for a long time that they sensed incredulous men there; because of them they wished to do nothing miraculous, from fear of converting them. But the fraud seems highly obvious to me. If it were true, why warn them about it? They ought, on the contrary, to harden us in our incredulity, hide in those bodies and not do things which could remove our blindness. You will answer that God forces them to that in order to make his Faith manifest. Yes, but I am not yet convinced nor obliged to believe that it is the Devil who does all this monkey business, because a man can do it naturally. Twisting one's face towards the shoulders? I've seen it done by Gypsies. Leaping? who doesn't do it, except paralytics? Swearing? one meets only too many who do that! Marking certain symbols on one's skin? either waters or stones will color our flesh that way without a miracle.

If the Devils are forced, as you say, to perform miracles in order to illumine us, let them do convincing ones. Let them take the towers of Notre-Dame of Paris, where there are so many unbelievers, and carry them unbroken into the country-

side of Saint-Denis to dance a Spanish safabande. Then we will
be convinced.

I also have observed that the Devil, who they say is such a
slanderer, never induces them (in the middle of their great
labors) to slander one another. On the contrary, they respect
each other greatly and have no wish to act otherwise, because
the first one to be offended would reveal the mystery. Why,
my Reverend Father, is your trial not begun because of the
crimes of which the Devil accuses you? The Devil (you say)
is the Father of lies. Then why, the other day, did you have that
Magician burned, who was accused only by the Devil? For I
answer like you: "the Devil is the Father of lies." Admit, admit,
my Very Reverend, that the Devil either tells the truth or lies
according to its usefulness to your malicious Fatherhood.
But, good Gods, I see that Devil shiver when holy water is
thrown on him. Is it such a holy thing that he cannot stand it
without horror? To be sure, it astonishes me that he has dared
to enclose himself in a human body which God has made in
His image, capable of seeing the Most High, has recognized as His
child through Baptismal regeneration, and has marked with
holy oils, the Temple of the Holy Ghost and the Tabernacle of
the holy Host. Where did he get the impudence to enter a place
which should be much more venerable to him than some water
over which prayers have merely been recited? But it must have
a good ending. I see the demoniac who throws a fit at the sight of
a Cross which is shown to him. O! mister Exorcist, how good
you are! Don't you know that there is no place in Nature
where there are no crosses, since all matter has length and width
and a cross is nothing but length matched with width? This
means that the Cross you hold is not a Cross because it is made
of mahogany; that other is not a cross because it is made of silver;
but both are Crosses because a width has been put across a
length. So if that demoniac has a hundred thousand lengths
and a hundred thousand widths which are all crosses, why show
her any new ones? However, you see that woman, whose lips
have been brought close to it by force, feign prohibition.
What a trick! Go ahead, take a good fistfull of switches and
whip me with them like a friend. For I pledge you my word that
if all the demoniacs whom one hundred blows of the strap per

day couldn't cure were condemned to be thrown into the water, none of them would drown.

I have already told you that I do not doubt the power of the Creator over his creatures. But unless convinced by the authority of the Church, to whom we should blindly extend our hands, I will continue to call all these great magical effects the gazette of fools or the "Credo" of those with too much faith.

2 FROM   *Malebranche*
Recherche de la Vérité (1674)

This philosopher and monk (1643-1715), famous in the history of thought as the great Christianizer of Cartesianism, provided a more carefully argued case against witchcraft than had Cyrano. His is among the earliest rationalist attempts to explain *witchcraft—not merely to deny it—which attempts to pick up where Weyer left off over a century before. The nub of Malebranche's explanation, the enormous power of the imagination plus the influence of certain soporific drugs, can also be found briefly in Cyrano (p. 117). Here, too, are the same middle-class contempt for the rustic shepherd, the same argument that the Devil has no real power over baptized Christians, and the same care to maintain orthodoxy.*

Malebranche represents the limits of mechanistic, Cartesian explanations of witchcraft and demonic possession in the seventeenth century; he is superior to the overrated work of Balthasar Bekker in Holland in the 1690's, which some scholars have mistakenly assumed dealt a crushing blow to the Devil and the witches. Malebranche and his psychology of groovelike traces in people's imaginations, reinforced primarily by hearsay evidence, may strike us as crude, but it did convince educated opinion in Louis XIV's France.

SOURCE. Malebranche, *Recherche de la Vérité* (1674), Book II, Part iii, Chapter 6; in *Oeuvres*, edited by G. Rodis-Lewis, Paris: Librairie Philosophique J. Vrin, 1962, I, pp. 370–376. Reprinted by permission of the publisher.

The strangest effect of the power of imagination is the dis-
orderly fear of the apparition of spirits, of enchantments, of
symbols, of the charms of Lycanthropes or Werewolves, and
generally of everything which is supposed to depend upon the
demon's power.

Nothing is more terrible or more frightening to the mind,
or produces deeper vestiges on the brain, than the idea of an
invisible power which thinks only about harming us and which
is irresistible. Speeches which reveal this idea are always heard
with fear and curiosity. Holding on to everything extraordinary,
men take bizarre pleasure in recounting these surprising and
prodigious stories about the power and malice of Witches, in
order to frighten both others and themselves. So it is not
astonishing if Witches are so common in some countries, where
belief in the Sabbat is too deeply rooted; where the most absurd
stories about spells are listened to as authentic; and where madmen and seers whose imagination has become disordered . . .
from telling these stories . . . are burned as real Witches.

I well know that some people will take exception to my attributing most witchcraft to the power of imagination, because
I know that men want to be made afraid, that they become angry
with those who want to demystify them, and that they resemble
imaginary sick men who respectfully hear and faithfully follow
the orders of doctors who diagnose baleful accidents for them.
Superstitions are not easily destroyed, and they cannot be attacked without finding a large number of defenders. It is easy
enough to prove that the inclination to believe blindly all the
dreams of Demonographers is produced and maintained by the
same cause which makes supersititous men stubborn. Nevertheless, that will not prevent me from describing in a few words
how, I believe, such opinions get established.

A shepherd in his fold after dinner tells his wife and children
about the adventures of the Sabbat. As his imagination is mod-
erately inspired by vapours from wine, and since he believes that
he has attended that imaginary assembly several times, he does
not fail to speak about it in a strong and lively manner. His
natural eloquence, together with the disposition of his entire
family to hear such a new and terrible subject discussed, should
doubtlessly produce strange traces in weak imaginations. It is

naturally impossible that a woman and her children not remain completely frightened, full, and convinced of what they have heard said. This is a husband, a father, who is speaking about what he has seen and done; he is loved and respected; why should he not be believed? This Shepherd repeats it on different days. Little by little the mother's and children's imagination receives deeper traces from it. They grow used to it, the fears pass, and the conviction remains. Finally they become curious to go there. With this intention they rub themselves with a certain drug, and go to sleep. Their hearts' disposition heats their imagination even more; and the traces which the Shepherd had formed in their brain open up enough to let them judge in sleep, as if they were present, all the movements of the ceremony which he had described to them. They arise, question each other and tell each other what they have seen. In this fashion they fortify in themselves the traces of their vision. The one with the strongest imagination, persuading the others best, fixes the imaginary history of the Sabbat within a few nights. So there are your finished Witches, made by the Shepherd. One day they will make many more, having a strong and lively imagination, unless fear prevents them from telling such stories.

Several times Witches of good faith have been found, who generally tell everybody that they have gone to the Sabbat, and who are so convinced of it, that although several persons watched them and assured them that they had not left their beds, they could not agree with their testimony.

Everybody knows that when ghost stories are told to children, they almost never fail to be frightened by them, and cannot stay without light and company. This is because when their brain receives no traces from any object present, the one which the story has formed reopens, often with enough force to represent before their very eyes the ghosts which have been described to them. However, they are not told these stories as though they were true. The stories are not told to them with the same tone of conviction, and sometimes they are told in a fairly cold and languid manner. So we should not be astonished if a man who thinks he has been to the Sabbat, and consequently talks about it in a firm voice and with an assured countenance, easily persuades some people who listen to him respectfully about all the circumstances which he describes, and thus transmits in their imagination traces similar to those which deceive him.

When men talk to us, they engrave in our brain traces similar to those which they possess. When they have deep traces, they talk to us in a manner which engraves deep ones in us; for they cannot speak without making us in some way similar to them. Children at their mother's breast only see what their mother sees. Even when they have become worldy-wise, they imagine few things of which their parents are not the cause, since even the wisest men conduct themselves more by the imagination of others, *i.e.*, by opinion and custom, then by the rules of reason. Thus in places where Witches are burned, a great number of them are found. Because in places where they are condemned to the fire, men truly believe that they commit witchcraft, and this belief is fortified by the speeches which are made about it. If one were to stop punishing them and were to treat them like madmen, then it would be seen in time that there would no longer be any Witches, because those who do it only in imagination (who are surely the greater number) would then abandon their errors.

It is indubitable that real Witches deserve death, and that even those who do it only in imagination ought not be treated as completely innocent; since ordinarily they are only persuaded to become Witches because they have a disposition of heart to go to the Sabbat, and have been rubbed with some drug to achieve their unhappy purpose. But by punishing all these criminals indifferently, common opinion is strengthened, imaginary Witches are multiplied, and so an infinity of people are lost and damned. It is thus right that many Parlements no longer punish Witches. There are many fewer of them in the lands of their jurisdictions; and the envy, hatred, or malice of evil men cannot use this pretext to destroy the innocent.

The dread of werewolves, or men transformed into wolves, is another pleasant sight. By a disordered effort of his imagination a man falls into this madness, so that he thinks he becomes a wolf every night. This mental disorder never fails to move him to perform every action which wolves do, or which he has heard that they do. Thus he leaves his house at midnight, runs through the streets, throws himself on a child if he meets one, bites him and maltreats him. The stupid and superstitious people imagines that in effect this fanatic becomes a wolf, because the unhappy man himself believes it and has said it secretly to some persons who have not been able to keep silent about it.

If it were easy to form in the brain the traces which persuade men that they have become wolves, and if one could run through the streets and commit all the ravages which these miserable werewolves do without having one's brain entirely scrambled—if this were as easy as it is to go to the Sabbat, in bed and without waking up—then these nice stories about the transformation of men into wolves would surely produce their effects, like those which are told about the Sabbat, and we would have as many werewolves as we have Witches. But the persuasion of being turned into a wolf supposes a cerebral confusion far more difficult to produce than that of a man who only thinks he goes to the Sabbat, *i.e.*, who thinks he sees unreal things at night and who, waking up, cannot distinguish his dreams from the thoughts which he has had during the day.

It is ordinary enough for some people to have fairly lively dreams at night and to be able to remember them exactly when awake, although the subject of their dream is not in itself very terrible. Thus it is not difficult for people to persuade themselves that they have been at the Sabbat, for that merely requires that their brain preserves the traces made there during sleep.

The chief reason which prevents us from taking our dreams for realities is that we cannot link our dreams with the things we have done during our wakefulness. By that we recognize that they were only dreams. But Witches cannot recognize in this way that their imaginary Sabbat is a dream. For one only goes to the Sabbat at night, and what happens at the Sabbat cannot be linked with other actions of the day. Thus it is morally impossible to undeceive them by that means. And it is not even necessary that the things which these supposed Witches believe they have seen at the Sabbat keep any natural order among themselves; for the more absurdities there were, and the more confusion in their order, the more real they then seem. It is thus sufficient for deceiving them that the ideas of the things of the Sabbat be lively and frightening, which cannot fail to happen, if we consider that they represent new and extraordinary things.

But for a man to imagine himself a cock, goat, wolf, or bull requires such a great disorder of the imagination that it cannot be ordinary; although such reversals sometimes happen, either by divine punishment, as the Scripture reports about Nebuchadnezzar, or by a natural surfeit of melancholy in the brain, of which examples are found in the Authors of Medicine.

I am persuaded that true Witches are very rare, that the Sabbat is only a dream, and that the Parlements who dismiss accusations of witchcraft are the most equitable. However, I do not doubt that Witches, charms, enchantments, etc., could exist, and that the demon sometimes exercises his malice upon men by special permission of a superior power. But Holy Scripture teaches us that Satan's kingdom is destroyed; that the Angel of Heaven has chained the demon up and has imprisoned him in the abyss, which he will only leave at the end of the world; that Jesus Christ has stripped off this strong weapon; and that the time has come when the Prince of the world [the Devil] has been expelled from the world.

He had reigned until the coming of the Saviour, and he still reigns, I grant, in places where the Saviour is not yet known. But he no longer has any right or any power over those who are reborn in Jesus Christ. He cannot even tempt them, unless God permits it; and if God permits it, it is in order for them to vanquish him. It is thus doing the devil too much honor to report Stories as marks of his power, as some new demonographers are doing, since these Stories make him formidable to weak minds.

Demons must be despised just like executioners must be despised. Man should tremble before God alone; His is the only power which must be feared. One must learn His judgments and His wrath, and not irritate Him by despising His Laws and His Gospel. One should be respectful when He talks, or when men talk to us about Him. But when men talk to us about the power of the devil, it is a ridiculous weakness to be frightened and troubled. Our trouble does honor to our enemy. He likes to be respected and feared, and his pride is satisfied when our spirit is bowed before him.

3 FROM   *Robert Mandrou*
Magistrates and Witches in Seventeenth-Century France

The product of nearly fifteen years of research, this book provides historians with the first truly thorough investigation of the decline of witchcraft persecution in any major European country. Mandrou has established the basic chronology of French persecution: after the last great wave of trials which covered all parts of the kingdom between 1580 and 1610 came an age dominated by a few famous trials of priests accused of bewitching entire convents of nuns, coincident with occasional regional outbreaks of the traditional, rural witchcraft. Finally, after 1660, French persecutions began to ebb definitively. The crucial point in this evolution was the decision of the Parlement of Paris, whose jurisdictional bounds included about half the kingdom, to stop persecuting persons accused of witchcraft sometime around 1640. But this new Parisian attitude was only slowly adopted by the other Parlements or sovereign courts of France. Often it had to be forced down the provincial judges' throats by royal action. Colbert intervened to stop death sentences for witchcraft at the Parlements of Pau, Rouen, and Bordeaux in the 1670's.

Mandrou's account of this evolution, which concludes with the new royal decree of July 1682 and its enforcement, is a full and rich narrative that pays considerable attention to the changing attitudes of the University of Paris, to the range of scientific opinion, of theology, and of medicine, as well as to the statements of the judges themselves. It is a detailed account giving us our first full answer to the question of how Europe's ruling classes came to change their opinions about witchcraft.

SOURCE. Robert Mandrou, *Magistrates and Witches in Seventeenth Century France*, Paris: Librairie Plon, 1968, pp. 548–564. Translated by Robert A. Wagoner, N.Y. State Maritime College. Reprinted by permission of the publisher.

It is readily admitted that the magistrates of the sovereign courts of France were among the intellectual élite of the kingdom. Both in the practice of their profession and their membership in the leading learned societies of the day, they came into contact with those who, like themselves, took an active part in the century's movement of ideas. Doctors, mathematicians, and theologians (and soon physicists) comprised their everyday intellectual environment. What was recognized about the Parisian magistracy—were we to judge only from the correspondence of Mersenne—was equally true, if to a lesser extent, of the great provincial capitals: Aix in the time of Peiresc; Dijon, with Philibert de la Mare and Jacques d'Autun; Rouen, with Bigot de Monville. Obviously, not every member of the judiciary shared the same degree of enthusiasm for intellectual curiosity. But the dialogues and debates that did occur are of greater importance than any labored attempt to estimate the precise number of participants. Certainly not every provincial capital had its Dupuy brothers or its scholarly lectures at the *bureau d'adresse,* no more than every court in session could produce an exemplary case of witchcraft or possession by an evil spirit, cases in which the postulates of Bodin, Boguet, and Lancre would be challenged and debated. But in every one of these provincial capitals, members of the judiciary stimulated the intellectual life of the community. They were in the forefront of the cultivated *"haute bourgeoisie"* which sought "to increase its learning by degrees and to raise its status little by little." In French society of the day these jurists were often men of science and promoters of intellectual curiosity, if not of scientific progress. Their extra-professional activities could very well fail to produce any radical changes in their judicial thinking and their professional practices. Although enlightened and eager for knowledge from libraries and learned socieities, they could also remain "buried in their ignorance and prejudices" the moment they walked into a courtroom.

But in contrast to this hypothesis are all the debates and arguments that characterized the great trials of the century as well as the reticences and hesitations of different courts when confronted with the problem. In each *parlement* the judges and their associates were obliged, sooner or later to come to grips with, and thrust into the open, this great confrontation between the positions of traditional jurisprudence, the ambiguous views of the theologians, the teachings of medicine, and the often vexing experience arising from a specific case under adjudication —a case that may have been previously judged by a court of first instance, or that of an urban convent reporting a wave of "possessions." The rallying of the courts to a new kind of jurisprudence gave proof, by the very slowness of the process, of the extent and difficulties involved in these confrontations. And by the same token, it demonstrated the uneven state of knowledge (in the broadest sense of the word) among the enlightened groups in the various provincial capitals, from Dijon to Rouen and from Bordeaux to Aix-en-Provence. The delays, uncertainties, hesitations, and resistance were evidence, not so much of prejudice and ignorance among the high court justices, as of the intellectual demands placed upon them. They could not separate their lives into two neatly divided compartments and continue judging witches and sorcerers in accordance with decrees previously handed down without debating and discussing them. Parisian judges were the first to do so, followed by those in the provinces, to the accompaniment of long and laborious debates that can be readily understood from the very nature and importance of the innovation.

These confrontations and judicial acts in which the highest courts overruled the decisions of lower courts, forcing them to accept, to some degree at least, a new concept of jurisprudence, revealed at the same time certain fundamental social cleavages. The great wave of prosecutions and slaughter that occurred in the closing years of the sixteenth century would be unintelligible without the judiciary's active espousal of popular beliefs concerning the Devil and his works. This point has been well established. It is valid for less important judges like Bouget, Le Loyer, even for Bodin himself (despite his other claims to fame), as for such parliamentary counselors as Pierre de Lancre. However, it is also quite clear that all trials were not regarded as equally important in the eyes of the judiciary. Epidemics of witch-hunting that ravaged entire provinces like Labourd, Lorraine, Burgundy, and Guyenne were always rural phenomena that sent peasant women by the dozens to be burned at the stake and which usually ended only for lack of willing victims. For a very long time these murderous events aroused little concern among the judiciary, whereas this kind of witchcraft went to the very heart of rural life, tragically exposing the existence in the village of a sorceress, simultaneously beneficent and maleficent, accepted and esteemed by the community as one possessing healing powers so long as some misfortune, denunciation, or zealous judge did not intervene. In fact, rural witchcraft in France was effectively condemened only after the great scandalous trials had taken place. But the latter occurred not as a result of intensified witch-hunts in the provinces, but from urban outbreaks of large numbers of persons allegedly possessed of evil spirits. Already in the last years of the sixteenth century, Martha Brossier had created a scandal in Paris at the very moment when Bodin's *Démonomanie* was reappearing in several editions published in Lyon and Paris, and when witch-hunts were proceeding apace in both Franche-Comté and Anjou. The notorious cases were those of the convents. The torment that afflicted a majority of young women in a community of Ursulines or *Hospitalières*, the accusations against priests, *directeurs de conscience*, traitors to their God and their conscience, provoked more public outcry than the wild ravings of peasant women poisoned by contaminated grains (*farines ergotées* and the often ruthless decisions of minor judges convinced they were fighting the good fight against the Prince of Darkness. There is no doubt that these events which required adjudication—even if they predicated the same premise of diabolical intervention—were something quite different. To be sure, popular beliefs in the role of the Devil were basically the same in town and country. It was even possible to find witches in the city who possessed scholarly treatises, like Della Porta, Agrippa, or worse, who consider themselves persons of lofty attainment in the magic arts, as did the cabinet maker Michel de Moulins. But the difference was both religious and social. In Marseilles as in Flanders, in Loudon as in Louviers, these young nuns, allegedly possessed by the Devil, belonged to the city's reputable families. In Chinon as in Loudon, relatives quickly intervened to demand exorcisms, investigations, and the intervention of authorities whenever they learned of these crises. The Ursulines of Loudon, who had *le diable au corps*, ex-

ploited the trances and the famous stigmatas displayed by Mother
Jeanne des Anges with a certain sense of publicity value, especially
after the death of Grandier. In short, from rural areas or urban
centers, the influence widely ascribed to the Evil One deployed
itself on victims who were no less willing to succumb to his
malevolent powers, but whose social rank precluded the traditionally harsh treatment meted out to poor village women convicted of being witches. This element of social differentiation
was further complicated by accusations of the regular clergy
leveled against priests, suborners and instruments of Satan at one
and the same time in an act of double treason. The accusation of
a priest, the perversion of a convent, quarrels among monks—
these constituent elements of the scandal inevitably lent an aura of
sensationalism to such events. . . . Public exorcisms then drew
large crowds. The fantastic revelations disclosed by these hysterical young women fanned the flames of scandal, whetted the
curiosity of countless individuals, and very soon gave rise to
doubts and scepticism.

Rural witchcraft and its counterpart in the convents did not
reflect the same kind of human reality. Contemporaries recognized the same obsession with the Devil, and his lust for perversion and destruction. They also saw clearly the enormous role
of imitation—even recitation—in the diffusion and repetition of
these demonopathic epidemics. The herdsman, described by Malebranche, recounted at eventide what he had heard a hundred
times around the fireside. The ordinary judge, at Saint-Claude or
at La Flèche, interrogated suspects and deliberated with his
Sprenger or Bodin under his sleeve to furnish him with the
questions and the answers. In like manner, Martha Brossier
imitated Nicole Obry, just as Jeanne des Anges and Madeleine
Bavent followed Madeleine de la Palud, and, at a much later
date, the young women of Landes copied the girls of Toulouse
in 1682.

But these similarities cannot conceal certain fundamental differences. The village sorceress, before being denounced, handed
over to justice, and, with rare exceptions, condemned to
death, was for a long time tolerated and accepted by her community. In a sense she found herself condemned more by laws,

civil and ecclesiastical, than by the group to which she belonged in the first place and to which she rendered great services, substituting for midwives and doctors and healing man and beast. This tacit complicity which was accidentally broken ("accident" being the word here for our ignorance) was a veritable mainstay in the structure of village life. Rural witchcraft was inseparable from this reality and from the overzealous ardor shown by judges in the prosecution and condemnation of witches. Yet nothing comparable can be discovered in the urban crises of demonopathic sorcery. They were a source of scandal, in every sense of the word and over a long period of time. Judges and enlightened opinion customarily acquiesced in the face of rural trials and their ensuing waves of repression that might ravage a small region, if not an entire province; but the prolonged reverberations occasioned by major outbreaks of the same phenomenon in the cities stands in sharp contrast. There was Loudun and Jeanne des Anges, of course, but that was not the most conclusive example. Thirty-five years after Gaufridi's death by torture, the traveler Monconys, visiting Provence, was concerned about Madeleine Demandols and called on her at her country house. Thirty years after the death of Marie Bucaille, eighteenth-century Norman scholars were still debating whether or not she had really been possessed by an evil spirit and were discussing the holiness of her works and her role in the religious life of the diocese of Coutances.

Witchcraft in the rural areas and diabolical torments in the cities thus illustrated in large measure the cultural cleavage between town and country, despite the surface similarities of their common beliefs. This demonopathic dichotomy thus coincided with the opposing positions of judges in the sovereign courts and those in courts of lower jurisdiction. Of course as late as the mid-seventeenth there were always royal counselors in the *parlements* who would affirm the reality of every alleged diabolical intervention. And inversely, there were certain minor judges who were scrupulous in their observance of traditional jurisprudence. Without going back to Boguet, who hesitated to have his treatise reprinted towards the end of his life, there is the good example of the judges from the court of Orléans consulting with theologians of the Sorbonne in 1625. Nevertheless, in the kingdom as a whole, it is quite clear that sovereign courts played the decisive role, led by the *Parlement de Paris*. Parisian jurists astonished enlightened opinion in the seventeenth century by the boldness of their views in this domain: witness the testimony of J. B. Thiers, J. D'Autun, Malebranche, and many others. Free and open discussions of "the miracles of Loudun" by judges, doctors, theologians, and scholars who gathered in the salons and libraries of Paris during the 1630's and '40's, were an essential element in this soul-searching reassessment. Men like Bignon, Servin, Molé, Mesmes, LeMaistre, Pithou, Sarrau, and Fabrot took the bold initiative of blazing the trail and renouncing a judicial practice adhered to for more than a century. In so doing, they clearly included both forms of sorcery in the same rejection of traditional jurisprudence, the rural and the urban variety. It was not possible to challenge the validity of chain reactions of "possessions by evil spirits" in city-based convents while simultaneously continuing to prosecute witches among the peasantry, inasmuch as both groups were victims, willing or not, of the same formidable foe bent on destroying the human race. But the dual nature of this judicial review explains in part the long delays that we mentioned. The new laws could not be imposed automatically throughout the country, following the initiative taken in Paris. By the same token, we can understand that this fundamental shift in judicial policy was the work of a closely-knit group of individuals—educated jurists, ever anxious to learn more, and closely associated with compatriots equally dedicated to the study and pursuit of knowledge. Their professional status undoubtedly placed them in a position of decision-making, but this revision of judicial policy implied far more than a new codification of laws, as noted with emphasis by Norman jurists in 1670, to wit: the refusal to prosecute accomplices of the crimes of Satan introduced, perhaps, "a new opinion contrary to the principles of Religion."

A NEW JURISPRUDENCE; A NEW MENTAL STRUCTURE

The debate that allowed the parliamentary justices to adopt this new jurisprudence on the crime of sorcery was nothing less than an ordeal of conscience, *une crise de conscience*, such as the judiciary experiences from time to time. But such occasions are rare, if it be true that the legal profession—traditionally bound by minute rules and regulations, even requiring a ritualistic vocabulary of its own—is more conducive to routine practices than to a continual re-examination of important principles. It is therefore all the more remarkable that seventeenth century judges of the sovereign courts undertook a task of such profound significance. Even if it required some notorious scandals to spark their critical sense, we must still be impressed by the bold manner in which they studied the judicial proceedings, analyzed the evidence, and rectified certain well-entrenched positions hallowed by a long tradition. We only wish that more evidence for this unprecedented step could be found in the records of their deliberations. The secret reports generally kept by most courts are, so to speak, silent on the subject of the internal discussions that eventually sanctioned the adoption of the new rule of law. But even this silence testifies to the extent of this crisis. The extensive polemical literature published during the great trials, as well as the dissertations by demonologists, are sufficient proof that this *crise de conscience* was not confined to the legal profession. It produced a wider debate in which jurists engaged in dialogue with theologians and doctors "to gain a clearer understanding of their religion" and to establish the new norms. The dialogue was of long duration, if we take Marescot's observations on Martha Brossier [1599] as one of its first, and chancellor Lalemant's reply to Pellot's questions [1671] as one of its last manifestations. These direct consultations, the lengthy dissertations, and the short *mémoires* for or against a defendant or witness, compensate in large measure for the lack of written reports on the secret deliberations of the courts. This abundant documentation enables us to discover the true dimensions of the debate and, more especially, the topics under discussion which alllowed the high court justices to adopt a new avenue of approach. There is little need to be reminded that the seriousness of the judicial reassessment was fully commensurate with the intellectual and spiritual atmosphere in which these intense discussions took place. To indicate once more the very close interdependence between a new judicial philosophy and a structural change in human mentality, it is sufficient to recall the alternatives that were decided upon in these discussions, the choices reached that finally allowed these judges to recover their peace of mind.

It is tempting to reduce everything to a distinction between the natural and the supernatural. Until the eighteenth century, polemicists continued to argue about the limits of natural possibilities and the kinds of behavior one may classify as human, basing their descriptions on testimony drawn from the trials. It is a legitimate temptation, provided the essential implications of this opposing position are clearly recognized. The earliest definitions of both exorcists and judges alike sought to establish a demarcation line between the natural and the supernatural. There were indeed acts that could not be accounted for solely on the basis of human capabilities: the intellectual power of a woman, for instance, who suddenly manifested a knowledge of foreign languages she had never before studied, or the phenomenon of levitation—a woman rising and moving about in the air, unsupported—or again the case of a woman remaining motionless while at the same time successfully resisting the efforts of three muscular men to move her. In the face of such duly observed facts as these, the innermost convictions of judges long remained undisturbed. Nevertheless, the question was finally brought up for discussion, not so much to challenge the validity of the testimony as to question the origins of these phenomena, the causes of the unusual powers or intelligence they revealed. It was a fundamental premise that any gift surpassing human capability came either from God or from the Devil. Theologians quickly reduced this latter, quasi-subsidiary alternative: the Devil can do only what God authorizes him to do among men. However, to punish the innumerable sins of mankind, God was reputed to have given great latitude to the Devil. Hence these supernatural phenomena betrayed the intervention of Satan in certain creatures. If possesseed, these creatures were no longer responsible individuals and should be delivered of their torment. If they were witches, they had solicited and obtained from the Prince of Hell these delegations of extraordinary powers enabling them to transgress the laws of nature. Everyone who took part in these discussions readily conceded that nature has its laws and that the crime of a sorcerer (or the misfortune of one possessed) began precisely at that point where nature's laws were transcended.

Here again—as with the attribution of the aforementioned phenomena to either God or the Devil—a corollary difficulty arose, creating a stumbling block for intelligent men anxious to know the causes of these tragic occurrences: nature obeys laws, but men have an imperfect understanding of those laws. Sixteenth-century philosophers and scholars wrote at length, and with good reason, about nature's secrets. Magicians, who repudiated any alliance with the Devil, boasted only of possessing some of those secrets, such as a knowledge of the virtues of medicinal plants and the "moral" properties of minerals, whereas great magicians claimed to have discovered the philosopher's stone. How then was it possible to draw a line between what is natural to man and what is beyond his capabilities? More than one disputant was caught on the horns of this dilemma. Those who were quickest to argue a ceaseless and indefatigable activity by the Devil in human affairs, resolved the question by describing as diabolical any activity not clearly and immediately intelligible. The celebrated Father Garasse was of this persuasion and owed a good part of his fame to what even his contemporaries labeled his "credulity." On the other hand, there were those who solved the problem by denying the reality of anything exceeding the feats of human capability as then understood. There were no *tours de force* or convulsions and contortions except those of buffons and entertainers. There was no feat of linguistic skill apart from the resemblance of Latin to French and a clever ability to guess the particular Latin required for exorcisms. For a Cyrano, nothing was true of men except what was true of the rank and file.

But between these two extreme positions—reflected in trials that followed the traditional practice of invoking the judgment of God, as in the ordeal by water, and the relentless interrogation of the accused until he finally succumbed to making the fatal confession—judges, theologians, and doctors were frequently at a loss to establish a boundary between the natural and the supernatural. Conversations with the dead, lycanthropy, the Witches' Sabbath—such subjects posed the same problem for them in a hundred different ways. That is why medical explanations found a receptive audience when doctors of recognized authority suggested the possibility of sickness or disease as a natural term to describe such phenomena. A new category of doctors intervened at that point, men no longer preoccupied with merely locating insensitive spots on the body, proof of Satan's complicity, but who demonstrated to judges the existence of feverish imaginings and deliriums—witches through imagination, as Malebranche put it.

The concept was slow in finding acceptance, for it posited another new idea. It was not merely a question of contrasting physical sickness and health, a concept generally accepted by seventeenth century doctors and the public at large so long as it dealt with such easily recognized disorders as stomach upsets and disturbances in the body's humors. The new alternative posed the notion of mental sickness and mental health. Even if, in the last analysis, these doctors attributed mental disturbances to an anomalous behavior of the humors (in their eyes the famous "suffocation of the womb" was due to such an occurrence), it is no less true that this new defintion posed an enormous problem for judges and even for theologians. The nocturnal journey to the Sabbath was shown to be something imaginary, as proved by a vigilant observer spending the night close to the sick person; thus was resolved the question of the migration of souls. Lycanthropy was also a dream, and a wide-awake dream, which took form as a result of chronological coincidences between mutilations of human beings and attacks by wolves. But the study of these cases (and of so many others) soon found itself enmeshed in questions of definition that were extremely delicate and controversial. Just where should the line be drawn between normality and abnormality in these difficult, uncharted areas under exploration? Father Surin saw nothing abnormal in the ecstatic trances of Mother Jeanne des Anges which the abbé d'Aubignac rejected *in toto*. Lemperière, a doctor in Rouen, pronounced the "possession" of Madeleine Bavent a manifest work of Satan, while his Parisian colleague, Yvelin, attributed her condition to no other cause then melancholy. To be sure, this widely recognized mental illness, characterized by states of languor and dark imaginings, linked to disturbances in the female psyche, provided the medical profession with good arguments to explain these deviations from the norm and did so, no doubt, for the very reason that it offered a defintion of a borderline condition between health and pathology. Unlike insane persons, *les aliénés d'esprit*, who were liable to forced detention, victims of melancholy were only temporarily disturbed individuals. There was no need to lock them up. Treat them gently, purge them of their offending humors, rid them of their pernicious fantasies, and perfect their Christian education—such measures should suffice to restore them to good health. Witches, especially the common rural variety, were not regarded as mad women. They deserved no other fate than to be given this simple therapeutic treatment.

The great *possédées*, however, did not precisely fit this definition since their cases presented still another complicating factor that gave rise, in turn, to a variety of explanations, especially what contemporaries called their *fourberie*, their trickery and deceit. Every debate surrounding these notorious "possessions" saw the reappearance of this accusation in the discussions between "*possessionistes*" and their opponents. The charge was often based on irrefutable arguments (according to the norms of seventeenth century medical science). Martha Brossier and Jeanne des Anges, as well as the young women of Toulouse in 1682, were taken by surprise by the stratagems of sceptical observers who, during an exorcism, replaced a holy relic with a piece of wood, a Bible with a *Malleus Maleficarum*, and holy water with a glass of water from the Garonne. And sometimes the doubters discovered some rather strange practices. Ten years after the great crisis in Loudun, Monconys, on his visit to Jeanne des Anges, removed with his fingernail a bit of paint from the stigmata of the Mother Superior. On such occasions, the experimenting sceptics, proud of their success, and doctors themselves, who could not imagine any connection between acts of simulation and their description of the disease of melancholy, arrived at the same conclusion of fraud and deceit on the part of the "so-called *possédées*". Because of their public nature and the apparent irrefutability of the evidence, these disclosures were extremely influential in reinforcing the notion of natural causation for all such phenomena and, by the same token, they cast great discredit upon the *possédées* themselves. As Marescot did in the case of Martha Brossier, the more critical judges itemized the factors attributable to sickness and those resulting from trickery: *Pauca a morbo; multa ficta.* Nothing was left for the Devil: *a daemone nulla.* For these critics, the domain of supernatural explanation vanished completely.

If the middle road, which was defined in the course of these debates, won the support of enlightened opinion (in which magistrates figured so prominently), it was largely because the various alternatives converged on the same conclusion, namely, a very sharp reduction in the role of the supernatural. Disciminating between the normal and the pathological, defining the nature of artful cunning, distinguishing melancholy from madness—all these elements in the study of judicial proceedings in witchcraft and sorcery played an important role and always, in the last analysis, pointed toward the same objective. They all sought to differentiate between the natural and the supernatural, between the physical and metaphysical. In juridical terms, when Colbert's counselors, at the time of royal interventions in Normandy, Guyenne, and Béarn, announced in 1670-72 the forthcoming publication of a general decree, they stipulated very clearly that this decree was to "establish the quality of proofs and witnesses" whose testimony could be used in reaching a judgment of condemnation—in other words, the kinds of evidence that could be introduced to prove supernatural intervention in these phenomena. In scientific terms, the formulation of an opinion by the Academy of Sciences thirty years later, sought to establish this distinction in a manner equally explicit. When LeBrun published his *History of Superstitious Practices Which Have Misled Peoples and Embarrassed Scholars,* [1701] he asked this learned body to give him their opinion of the book by way of an endorsement. The Academy's statement, signed by Fontenelle and Malebranche, declared the work "well reasoned" and stated that "the principles which are set forth to distinguish the natural from the unnatural are sound." The establishment of this new jurisprudence belongs to the effort, slowly realized in the seventeenth century, to surmount the metaphysical obstacle impeding the development of a science and a mode of thinking based upon reason. It constitutes an example—perhaps the finest one—of a crisis of conscience which, in turn, reflected a crisis of intellectual growth.

To put it differently, an examination of this gradual transformation of thought enables us to define, in part at least, what is meant by the expression *progrès des lumières*, the growth of enlightenment—not only scientific progress (the scientific truths that so fascinated the eighteenth century)—not only the battle of ideas to which each great philosopher brought his contribution, discussing and going beyond his predecessors—but actually a sweeping re-evaluation of conscience and intellect that called into question mankind's traditional modes of thinking and feeling, man's age-old mental structures providing visions of the universe inherited from a distant past and accepted as valid by certain groups, indeed by societies throughout the world. The judiciary's abandonment of accusations of witchcraft clearly reflected a revision in this ancient order of things. Instead of a vision of the world where men live under the daily surveillance of the God of the Last Judgment (who is conscious of their slightest actions) and are helped by this same God who is a God of love, and are constantly assailed at the same time by the Prince of Darkness—instead of this vision, the new intellectual milieus substituted another concept wherein divine surveillance became more remote and intervention by God or the Devil in human affairs infinitely more rare. In this vision of the world, God and Satan were certainly inseparable. It was for this reason that Norman magistrates saw in the new jurisprudence a threat to the very principles of religion. No doubt they were also thinking of the more categorical negations of free-thinkers who, in private confessions of their innermost thoughts, ventured to deny the existence of either God or the Devil. But we are properly concerned here with the middle position, defined as well by Jacques d'Autun or Malebranche as by André du Val. While avoiding radical departures from orthodoxy (which was still the practice of only a few thinkers), the middle position embodied the fundamental change. For even in this outlook, the shift was a fundamental one. God and Satan ceased their daily intervention in the natural course of things and in the ordinary life of human beings. This view restored an autonomy to man and nature which the previous confusion between the natural and supernatural, as was readily admitted, had made impossible. However, it was the Devil's intervention that was most emphatically denied since that was the issue continually at stake in the denunciations, trials, and debates and was the primary source of apprehension.

Refuting the metaphysical obstacle resulted then in de-emphasizing the role of Satan, in reducing the frequent interventions of the Demon in earthly affairs. This meant not merely the abandonment of a concept of physics in part animistic, and the establishment of another concept in which natural causes played the predominant role. The debate was not simply a confrontation between scientific minds eager for proofs and explanations based on more solid evidence and more demonstrable facts. The celebrated meetings that prepared the way for the founding of the Academy of Sciences might create a false impression. Whatever the role played by scholars and scientists with their sense of the comparative (if not of the experimental)—a fine example of which is found in the correspondence of Mersenne and Peiresc concerning the witch of Sens—we must add yet another dimension to this picture. The disappearance of Satan was also, and perhaps most importantly, a disappearance of fear. Confidence in explanations "that do not go beyond the limits of natural forces" predicated an important emotional basis. A kind of human "generosity" emboldened these thinkers who were anxious to exhaust all possibilities of natural causation, within the range of human reason, before invoking the intervention of "unseen powers."

The human attitude, both intellectual and emotional, that was rejected by these enlightened groups, is exemplified in the extreme case of Father Surin. This constantly tormented *directeur de conscience* of Jeanne des Anges was engaged in a continual struggle with the Tempter, to the point of physical exhaustion and bodily illness, sometimes causing deep concern among his ecclesiastical superiors. In contrast to this kind of anguish, the rejection of the metaphysical by such enlightened contemporaries as Claude Pellot and P. Lalemant remained purely and simply a determination to find explanations for human behavior (and other phenomena) that ruled out the terrifying fantasies intimately associated with the traditional view of human destiny. Against these fevered imaginings which simultaneously engendered fear and error, enlightened minds affirmed a new serenity of spirit. Other (social) terrors could, of course, move in, pick up the torch, and generate new anxieties. But these men had succeeded in overcoming their fear of the Devil.

But again we must emphasize that all this was no easy matter. The decline in the number of sorcery trials, following the more notorious cases, was a slow process of the kind accompanying any difficult achievement. Among the group of advanced thinkers most likely to accept innovations, doubts and reservations or postponements of decisions were more common than collective agreements or frank and enthusiastic endorsements by the majority. Among those jurists whose way of life and social prominence placed them in the center of the century's intellectual life, this new approach was slow to gain acceptance. The more obstinate judges eventually had the new jurisprudence forced upon them by royal authority. Moreover, formulating the legal terminology was such a delicate matter that it could not be spelled out with precision either by the *Parlement de Paris,* which had initiated the legislation, or by the chancellor or the king in his council. It took nearly half a century—or more than a generation—before there was general acceptance of this new relationship between men, the world, and God. The range of problems arising from a simple refusal to prosecute a peasant accused of having caused the death of a goat through a pact with the Devil, was certainly a basic cause for the slowness of this process. The many scholarly discussions (on the coldness of air, the cause of the winds of the sea, the nature of mineral waters) which preoccupied Renaudot's colleagues in their lectures and papers at the *bureau d'adresse,* did not broach the question, which arose at these trials, of the nature of the whole order of the universe. They did not answer the question that demonologists and their adversaries never ceased to speculate on and mull over again and again, namely: to whom must we attribute facts that clearly transcend the forces of nature? A scientific, rational analysis of these phenomena was slow in getting under way because of the need to overcome enormous obstacles. Everything had to be re-examined. It was necessary to reinterpret the statements of the Old Testament condemning magicians to death in the time of Moses and to restore the discreet practice of exorcism. It was necessary to undertake a close observation of those "possessed of the Devil" and of their "contortions" in order to distinguish between mental illnesses and female disturbances (*"maladies de mère"*) in those cases where uncritical witnesses preferred to see only the hand of the Devil. It was also necessary to be willing to consult doctors on other matters than merely the location of *marques insensibles*, insensitive areas of the body, and to impose rigorous standards on the inventory of admissible evidence, eliminating idle talk, public gossip, and the charge of "evil reputation," in order to arrive at a precise definition of a specific crime. And there was the need to abandon the appeal to God's final judgment, the ordeal by drowning. . . . Consequently, these magistrates of the sovereign courts who reformed their methods of investigating and forming judgments, who assimilated into their thinking a better understanding of medical knowledge and a greater familiarity with Holy Writ and the commentaries of theologians—these men held a preeminent position in the advancement of rationalism in seventeenth-century France. Their new interpretation of diabolical possessions and fantasies associated with the Sabbat was indeed a rational attempt—scientific in every sense of the word—to account for phenomena traditionally explained as the exclusive work of the Devil. The difficulties encountered in achieving this victory demonstrate how a collective shift of such magnitude could only be accomplished slowly and painfully, at the cost of numerous setbacks and prolonged delays. It success was for a long time precarious and uncertain, even while the movement gained fresh support and adherence. It is the enormous distance that separates the individual quest of a Montaigne, who learned how to maintain reason within himself (*"raison garder"*) and that collective adventure which, in the words of Gaston Bachelard, a "spiritual revolution" represents.

PART FIVE

Recent Perspectives on Witchcraft

What unites the following three examples of recent research into the central problems of the history of European witchcraft, and at the same time separates them from other modern writers on the subject—from Hansen in 1900 to Trevor-Roper in 1967 or Mandrou in 1968—is their common starting-point. All three are primarily interested in the witch's view of herself and of her world; all three are trying to understand witchcraft from within. The first of these three authors has said it most succinctly:[1]

"This is the essential problem for those who investigate witches and witchcraft: what is the nature of reality in a world where witches exist? Above all, what do those who believe themselves to be the victims of witchcraft believe to be real? Much more is known about sorcery from the point of view of those who believe in witches than from the witches themselves. And we have to analyse the mentalities of such people: the mentalities of whole communities gripped by a specific fear, not simply individuals convinced of their own unnatural powers."

Of course, this is an extremely difficult procedure. Witches were mostly illiterate and, like many other early heresies, left no surviving apologetic writings. We must study them through the bent prism of their accusers' words, or at best by means of more or less voluntary

[1] Julio Caro Baroja, *The World of the Witches*, translated by O.N.V. Glendenning, Chicago, 1964, p. xiii.

confessions hastily scribbled down by some clerk during their interrogations. The problem of understanding them in their own terms is almost insoluble, precisely for just such reasons.

Nevertheless, some attempts have been made to escape this dilemma. In our first selection, a Spanish anthropologist examines the witches' testimony primarily through various psychoanalytical techniques. In the second selection, an Italian historian examines the transformation of a certain kind of folklore into orthodox witchcraft, utilizing a rich fund of fairly voluntary confessions. In the final selection, a French historian draws analogies from the psychology of peasant revolts to help explain both the tenacity and the limitations of witchcraft beliefs.

These examples do not exhaust the possible ways of examining the network of witchcraft beliefs from within. Caro Baroja, for example, suggests that some controlled experimentation with the hallucinatory drugs of the nightshade family could provide valuable insights (p. 155). It is also possible that have not exhausted the pictorial or documentary evidence about witches, as well as the biological evidence (witches were undernourished peasants, prone to hallucinations). The examples presented here can and should be supplemented; their common presupposition, that witchcraft needs to be studied primarily from the point of view of the witch instead of the point of view of the judges, seems to be the best way to open up new vistas on this subject.

FROM   *Julio Caro Baroja*
            The World of the Witches

First published in Spanish in 1961, this is certainly the best one-volume history of European witchcraft in existence today. The author, a well-known anthropologist and social historian, has specialized in studies of the Basques. This people has one of the oldest and most continuous traditions of witchcraft beliefs running from the Middle Ages into the twentieth century; Caro Baroja has been able to collect contemporary as well as ancient evidence about Basque witches, and thus possesses an unusually secure and important regional base from which to work.

His book begins and ends with psychological descriptions of various aspects of the witch's world, but its core is a rapid yet subtle history of witchcraft from Greco-Roman antiquity up to the Enlightenment. The result is a successful combination of history and psychology, and a sharp criticism of what he considers the rigid and oversimplified approaches of previous scholars. Here, in his concluding section, he examines the problem of demoniacal neuroses, rejects the notion of "contagion" or mass hysteria, gives qualified support to the idea of "mythomania" in witchcraft witnesses, and finally examines the witches themselves, their opiates, and their powerlessness in the everyday world.

THE VIEWS OF PSYCHIATRISTS

Some societies are certainly more prone to belief in witchcraft than others. Dr. Fortune, in his book *The Sorcerers of Dobu* (New York, 1932) has shown, for instance, that groups of human beings in Dobu live in a world where spells play a vital

SOURCE. Julio Caro Baroja, *The World of the Witches*, translated by O.N.V. Glendenning. Chicago and London: University of Chicago Press and George Weidenfeld & Nicolson, Ltd., 1964, pp. 247–253 and 254–257. Reprinted by permission of publishers.

part in every aspect of their existence. And when the civil authorities in Guipúzcoa, Vizcaya and other old parts of Europe complained of the number of spells which were upsetting the inhabitants, and asked for legal action to be taken, they were admitting the full significance of magic in those places and at that time. The misfortunes and illnesses of individuals, and of society as a whole, were ascribed to spells. But judging from historical example, it was the *victims* of spells, not witches and sorcerers, who usually caused official steps to be taken about witchcraft— although this is contrary to what is found in primitive societies. In fact, the *passive belief* of those who are bewitched does more to create a social climate like that of Guipúzcoa in the fifteenth or sixteenth century, than the *active belief* of the sorcerers. The same is true of the more important individual cases at a later date.

In Spain, for instance, Charles II was convinced that he was bewitched, and nearly the whole of society, from the highest aristocrats to the lowest plebs in Madrid, accepted the idea and spread it about. The nature of the spells and the personality of the sorcerer remained obscure and anonymous. And those who tried to relieve the unfortunate king by exorcisms and other processes were later tried and condemned by the Inquisition.

Such societies are fair game for those who are interested in mental sickness and psychical disturbances, particularly if magic —as Malinowski thought—is primarily based on feelings of frustration and impotence. The magician may well be driven to act by such feelings; and the victims may suffer from persecution mania. In societies which believe in magic such phenomena would be particularly important factors. Non-religious communities are prone to a variety of complexes.

The distinction between active and passive beliefs is also useful as an aid to understanding the psychiatrist's point of view. In the first half of the nineteenth century, psychiatrists were already putting forward the theory that witchcraft, at least in the major witch-trials, was a kind of mass hysteria. Calmeil, in his important book entitled *De la folie*, collected together quite a number of examples of what he called "Demoniomania" to support this view. More recent psychiatrists have been able to draw on his large fund of material. However, a clear distinction has never really been made between the demoniacal neurosis of those who are bewitched, possessed or liable to fits on the one hand, and witches and sorcerers on the other. The psychopathology of the witch herself remains blurred, while that of the other people involved has been clarified. Richet, for instance, did not hesitate to compare the chronic cases of hysteria which Charcot studied in La Salpetrière with the "demoniacally possessed of the past." These cases of hysteria were also found to produce symptoms remarkably like those of witches. They lost the sense of feeling in parts of their bodies for instance. This was the starting-point for Richet's study of witchcraft as a "contagious disease," in which he also discussed cases of possession in some detail.

Subsequently, A. Marie drew attention to the link between the incidence of witchcraft cases and long periods of moral and physical suffering. But Marie, inevitably, concentrated on later cases where possession by the Devil is all-important rather than on cases of witchcraft proper. The same is true of other students or "demonpaths," as they came to be called. The views of psychiatrists of the late nineteenth and early twentieth centuries are, in fact, diametrically opposed to those of the theologians. But it should be pointed out that they, too, used early texts in a rather cavalier manner and were not always very scholarly in their approach to documentary sources. The practical work they carried out on living persons was, in reality, much more useful than their researches into cases of the past. The examples they gave of modern women from urban backgrounds who had feelings of anxiety, accompanied by the sensation that there was somebody with them, are particularly interesting. On occasion, such feelings are followed by voluptuous sensations, so that there is medical evidence for "succubi," although I do not know whether such cases are at all common.

There are also one or two other isolated cases which can be linked with witches, or with the physical characteristics ascribed to them, such as the lack of feeling in certain parts of the body. But, unfortunately, there is no fully elaborated analysis with hospital and clinical evidence. For this reason I must insist that the theory of *contagion* amongst the victims of repressive measures against witches and sorcerers can only be accepted with strong reservations. In reality, the most obvious cases of contagion that can be studied in the light of modern psychiatric research are those of the judges and witnesses at witch-trials. In the first place the latter are responsible for such information as we have and, what is more, they also provide first-hand documentation about themselves. I hope that earlier chapters of this book will already have demonstrated this adequately. But it is not only in dealing with the psychiatric problems involved in the study of witchcraft that the mentality of judges and witnesses is of the first importance. The same approach is valid when legal problems are under examination.

On this particular point (in connexion with the judges) it is worth recalling an essay of Jules Valles. In the view of this forceful writer and member of the Commune, *books* were the motivating force behind the vast majority of human actions. And he wanted to replace the rule "cherchez la femme," dear to historians and psychologists, by "cherchez le livre." The extent to which books influence or have influenced both individual and collective action, is indeed remarkable. A clear example of this in the history of witchcraft is the case of the *Malleus Maleficarum*. The views it advanced spread rapidly through Italy, Spain, France and countries in the north of Europe. Both Catholics and Protestants were influenced by it. And the more learned was the judge in charge of a trial, the more notice he took of it. Pierre de Lancre was undoubtedly more erudite than Alonso de Salazar y Frías. And King James I of England was no bad scholar. But pedants with power in their hands, supported by a whole arsenal of authorities and the opinions of other pedants like themselves, can be dangerous; more especially if there is a mass of people only too willing to give in to their ideas and pay tribute to their pedantry, because they are too frightened to do anything else. And this is how the pedant in authority comes to judge real or supposed witches, and is ready to condemn any spell which is said to have been cast.

Now let us turn to others who are hostile to the accused, namely the witnesses. Here the practical experiences of psychiatrists are of far greater value than in the case of witches themselves.

THE WITNESSES

It was E. Dupré, a doctor working in Paris at the beginning of this century and a specialist in forensic medicine with many scholarly books to his credit, who first used the word "Mythomania." He used it to describe the pathological tendency to lie and invent imaginary stories which he had observed in a large number of cases in the course of his professional work.

A person who is "mythomaniac," even though he may lie deliberately, finally comes to believe what he has said. The majority of those who do this are either children or mentally retarded. In children, continued lying does not necessarily indicate a pathological state, whereas in adults it does. In children or abnormal adolescents mythomania is most frequently associated with vanity, maliciousness and precocious sexual appetites. In cases where the mythomane tends to be vain or malicious, a suggestion from outside may well set him off on a particular course of action. This form of mythomaniac activity prompted from outside was what particularly interested Dupré and most concerns us here. As a result of auto-suggestion, Dupré tells us, a number of children have given utterly false testimony in courts of law, with a good deal of imaginary detail, more particularly about supposed attempts to outrage their innocence.

Dupré also tells us (after describing several cases of mythomania involving auto-suggestion) that it is frequently the conversation of people around the child who is supposed to have been attacked, or the questions of members of his family, which ultimately forms the substance of his accusations.

"In spite of their surprise and indignation, which restrains them somewhat, friends, and above all, the family, anxious to know all the details of the attack, the time, the place, the motives and so on of the criminal act, bewilder the perturbed and embarrassed child with their questions; they ascribe his confusion to shame or repentance, and without knowing it put into his mouth the very answers they are so anxious to hear. In this view, the whole tale is prepared and arranged, learnt by heart by the child so that nothing can shake him from it. The child wishes not to forget anything when telling it, and so sticks rigidly to the version now imprinted in his mind. If he does add anything it is only new material suggested to him in the course of further interrogations."

Other aspects of evidence and its relative value in criminal enquiries have been studied by doctors helping with police investigations. These could be mentioned at this point, since they would show how certain of the witch-trials have been used as the basis for a scientific study of the use of evidence to prove guilt in criminal cases. According to a number of experts, witnesses who are genuinely concerned to speak the truth (let alone those who are not) have a tendency to exaggerate or even lie when giving evidence.

In Paris or other capital cities today, judges and lawyers can be shocked by crude or obscene stories from young perverts or psychologically disturbed adolescents. But in older societies with a deeper respect for the mysterious, crudeness and obscenity could be seen quite simply as an aspect of magic, or as being inextricably linked with the power and activities of the Devil. In the evidence given by young boys and girls in the witch-trials there are always, or nearly always, numerous mentions of the most obscene occurrences. It is often difficult to see exactly how much of this was put into the minds of the children by their relatives or the judges, although, at times, the influence of the family or the judges is clear, as in the case of the witches at Fuenterrabía.

Margaret Murray, and other authors who take a similar line (not to mention modern Devil-worshippers who celebrate Black Masses in large hotels or in luxurious, air-conditioned houses complete with central heating), seem to be harking back to those who accepted the reality of everything connected with witchcraft in earliest times. When they speak of the survival of the cult of the Horned-God and that sort of thing, they are, in fact, rejecting all serious, factual investigation of the subject, without religious bias (and the sixteenth century is far enough away from us for this), in favour of more or less arbitrary archaeological fabrications. They also fail to take into account writers who treat the witch-trials as an essentially legal problem and discuss them in a lively and interesting manner from that point of view

There have been a number of instances of this legal approach recently, and the witch-trails have often been compared with the methods used to repress certain present-day political activities. Arthur Miller, for example, has written a successful play about the trials of the witches of Salem, which is a covert attack on the political tribunals operating in the United States at the time when it was written. Miller, in reality, does little more than give artistic shape to the conclusions of scholars who, for a variety of reasons, see the problem of witchcraft in terms of a vast miscarriage of justice resulting from an abuse of power.

It is, however, important to distinguish between two kinds of persons who have approached the witch-trials from this standpoint. On the one hand, those like Alonso de Salazar, Father Spee and other Catholic lawyers and ecclesiastical authorities, who were trying to find a solution to a serious problem. On the other, those who, many years later, used the mistakes of the Catholic Church and the Pope, to question their authority. Protestant historians, like Lea, used them in this way, and so did Catholic theologians who disagreed with the official views of the Church, like Canon Döllinger. Finally, at the end of the nineteenth century and beginning of the twentieth, rationalists went still further: Jules Baissac, for instance, and the writer whose pseudonym was "Jean Français." On very little foundation— these writers declare—a vast legal structure was erected by the Catholic Church, which was really to blame for the injustice done—although Protestsants did not hestiate to use the same methods. This kind of view may seem rather puerile today. In any case what we really want to know are the basic facts which gave rise to the legal mistakes. There is nothing new in inventing a crime and finding people guilty of it in retrospect, nor in making laws which are unrelated to real facts, and refer only to imaginary crimes dreamed up by those who make the laws or by unreliable witnesses. There are legal abuses into which man or rather society has fallen on many occasions both before and since the Middle Ages. But since we are living in a period when the same abuses are again rearing their ugly heads, we may well understand our subject the better for considering the political trials of today. For life tells us more about

history than history about life. Whenever there is an abuse
there are real circumstances which give rise to it.

THE PERSONALITY OF THE WITCH

At last we come to the witch herself, or the person who thinks
she is a witch. What are the characteristcs of these followers of
Simeta and Canida? Sometimes they are, like Celestina, pro-
curesses and go-betweens. Sometimes, an altogheter stranger
type of person emerges, slightly mad, weird, but not wholly
improbable, and perhaps nothing like so fantastic as she is made
out to be. The witch of country areas is usually an old woman,
an outsider, who is both feared and despised, and who has some
knowledge of quackery. She foretells the future from time to
time, and maybe finds consolation in the dream world which
certain European herbs can give her. Without accepting the tall
stories about maleficent powders, ointments made from toads and
so on, which have so often been uncritically repeated, it must
be admitted that the witch could often have used drugs to induce dream-states in others and in herself.

. It was from the plants of the nightshade family, like belladonna,
henbane and the common thorn-apple, that most of the sleep-
inducing drugs used in Europe were made. Further east scopelia
was used, and mandragora in the Mediterranean. There were a
number of ways of inducing sleep with these plants. Sometimes their leaves were boiled, sometimes they were smoked.
Drinks were concocted and an ointment was made from them,
which was probably the basis of the unguents so often referred
to in the witch-trials. Sleep induced in these ways brought with
it fantastic dreams. In Europe today, and in central Europe
more particularly, poor people still use plants of the nightshade
family as an opiate. They take them for pleasure since wines
and liquors are usually beyond their means, and they are sometimes used to strengthen weak beer, although laws have been
passed to prevent this. Specialists maintain, in fact, that nightshade is a far more harmful opiate even than hashish. And another great disadvantage of it is the depressing nature of the

dreams it usually produces. We have already found references to the use of this sort of opiate in connection with witchcraft in sixteenth century writers. But knowledge of it was by no means confined to men with medical knowledge at that period. Authors of works of literature also seem to have been aware of its effects, and some of them realized, as early as that, that it could be the explanation of the belief that witches could fly. In a play called *Lo que queria el Marqués de Villena (What the Marquis of Villena wanted)* by Rojas Zorrilla, for instance, we find the following piece of dialogue:

MARQUIS   .. Others believe that witches can fly.

ZAMBAPALO .. And can't they?

MARQUIS   .. Certainly not, you ignorant fellow.

ZAMBAPALO .. Since I'm no specialist in these matters, I must ask you what happens.

MARQUIS   .. They all rub themselves with ointment.

ZAMBAPALO .. And then what?

MARQUIS   .. The ointment, which is an opiate made from henbane given them by the Devil, sends them to sleep, and they dream such a dream that they think they are not dreaming at all. And since the Devil has great power to deceive, he makes them all dream the same dream. And that is why they think they are flying through the air, when they are really fast asleep. And although they never fly at all they think, as soon as they wake, that they have all been to see the calf, and all visited the fields at Baraona. When, by God, in reality, more than two of them have been sleeping in their rooms with the ointment on them.

If one has only a very remote and academic idea of what the Devil is like, and finds it difficult to imagine his omnipresence, I suppose one really ought to experiment and try one or two of these opiates, to see what kind of effect they have. But although I would be in a better position to discuss this point if I had tried them, I have never been able to bring myself to do it. I can only apologise for this failure on my part at such an important juncture in my book.

It is these opiates, then, and not flying brooms or animals, which carry the witch off into a world of fantasy and emotion. And it is a pity that modern psychologists have not had a chance to examine some of the women in question. They would almost certainly have found them to be rather insignificant people in their normal environment, who wanted to be far superior to, and very different from, what they really were. Ultimately they came to believe they had the status they desired. They were perhaps rather like Emma Bovary in their own particular way, but living in a rather different kind of society from the lower middle-class background of Flaubert's character.

The few reliable descriptions of witches which have come down to us are nearly all of people with an overdeveloped sense of their own importance, quite convinced that a woman with a humble town or country background could do the most remarkable things. They usually started their activites when they were middle-aged or old, although there have been some cases in which demoniacal powers developed early in life.

In any case, a woman usually becomes a witch after the intial failure of her life as a woman; after frustrated or illegitimate love affairs have left her with a sense of impotence or disgrace. This, in turn, drives her to use improper means to achieve her ends, although this does not always involve the work of the Devil in the Chrstian sense of the word. Her situation changes as she grows older, and no longer has any strong sensual desires. In old age, perhaps, her only satisfaction is to see younger women go the same way as she, living a life of false or inverted values. For them evil becomes good; the crooked, straight. What is public loses its importance, and what is private and carried out in the strictest secrecy becomes significant. The sorceresses of antiquity did, in fact, form a female secret society. But I believe that field work is needed to prove that this feminine witchcraft is quite different from Devil-worship, although the two are often inextricably linked. It also seems to me that the important thing to bear in mind when discussing the two is the distinction between passive and active beliefs. Many of the documents quoted in the past by historians and students of folklore need to be reinterpreted, and many questions re-examined, from a sociological and philosophical rather than from a religious viewpoint.

I do not doubt that Black Masses and similar activities still take place today, and that there are one or two cases of Devil-worship from time to time. But I believe that the people involved nowadays are usually fairly sophisticated in spite of their tendency to be self-important, and their morbid interest in anything psychopathic—sexually psychopathic particularly. They are, in fact, very different in every way from the witches of rural areas in medieval, sixteenth and seventeenth-century Europe. And they are not in the least like those unfortunate sick people who were put to death at that period because nobody knew what was wrong with them.

I make this last point with the so-called werewolves more particularly in mind. For lycanthropy is no more than an illness in reality. It has, for some time past, been studied by specialists in mental diseases, and has recently been discussed (like sadism and masochism) by Eisler, in a posthumous work, in relation to Jungian psychology.

In conclusion, it seems to me, as a historian, that witchcraft makes one feel pity more than anything else. Pity for those who were persecuted, who wanted to do evil yet could not do it, and whose lives were generally frustrated and tragic. Pity, too, for the persecutors who were brutal because they believed that numberless dangers surrounde them. Perhaps we are in a better position nowadays to appreciate the feelings of the people involved, who discovered one day that they had a devilish power in them, or were subject to the devilish power of a close enemy who had lived near them for years, watching and hating. For ours is no period of calm, with an optimistic view of public morality and religious philosophy and beliefs. It is an age of existentialism and an existentialist way of life, which leads man to break down the barriers and conventions and face up to his own *angst*.

It is not, after all, so hard for us to understand those men and women. Their age, like ours, was an age of *angst*. Only their idea of reality radically separates them from us.

2 FROM   *Carlo Ginzburg*
I benandanti: Richerche sulla stregoneria e sui
culti agrari tra Cinquecento e Seicento

*A genuinely pioneering study, based upon a few dozen trials in
the Inquisitorial archives of the Venetian province of Friuli, Ginzburg's book marks a significant advance in the historiography of
witchcraft. His main thesis is the mutation of belief in a rural population under the steady and purposeful cross-questioning of the Inquisition. The* benandanti *or "go-gooders" were men and women whose
amniotic membranes had been preserved after their birth, and now
hung round their necks as an amulet. They were fated to "go out" at
night, while apparently asleep, at certain times of the year in order to
battle the witches. This ritual battle would determine the fate of the
coming harvest, for the* benandanti *were defenders of fertility against
the witches, who caused bad weather and sterility. But gradually, between 1620 and 1650, the "go-gooders" began to vary their stories
under questioning. Inquisitors who could not understand how a real
Christian could "go out" while asleep, like witches, and do battle with
witches without being witches themselves, gradually persuaded the*
benandanti *that they really were witches themselves. Ginzburg has
provided the first concrete example of how rural folklore could be
transformed into ordinary witchcraft and how a harmless fertility cult
ended up accusing itself of performing black magic.*

The polemics of the Enlightenment (exemplified in Italy by
Tartarotti) were obviously, and rightly uninterested in the
witches' confessions. What mattered was only the demonstration of the barbarity and irrationality of the persecutions, and

SOURCE. Carlo Ginzburg, *I benandanti: Richerche sulla stregoneria e sui
culti agrari tra Cinquecento e Seicento*, Turin: Guilo Einaudi Editore S.P.A.,
1966, pp. xiii-xv and 20–24. Reprinted by permission of publisher and author.

the witches' stories were liquidated as absurd fantasies or as confessions extorted by the ferocity and superstition of the judges. The earliest attempts at interpretation came in the second half of the nineteenth century with erudite researches in which the accused witches' confessions were generally seen as the fruit of hallucinations derived from ointments made from narcotic substances, or else from pathological conditions, especially hysteria. But the most serious and best-documented studies were particularly concerned—often with a subdued anticlerical or anti-Catholic polemic, more or less explicit—with explaining the events and the mechanism of the persecution.

A real interest in the beliefs of the witches or supposed witches . . . came only with the researches of the English Egyptologist, Margaret Murray. A disciple of Frazer and thus interested in the problems of magic and of "primitive" mentality, she did not limit herself to stressing the interest of accused witches' confessions from an ethnological or folkloristic viewpoint. Paradoxically overturning positions (but instead of a reasoned position, one should speak of an instinctive sympathy), she re-evaluated the worth (in the positivist sense of the *external* worth of a source) of their confessions. According to Murray, the covens described by the accused were real, and witchcraft was a very old religion, a pre-Christian fertility cult, in which the judges . . . could only see a diabolical perversion. This thesis, which contained the proverbial kernel of truth, was formulated in a totally uncritical manner. In addition, her reconstruction of this supposed fertility cult was built on the base of very late trials, in which the assimilation of the Inquisitorial schema (Sabbats, sexual union with the Devil, etc.) had already taken place. However, despite these substantial defects, Murray's thesis, rejected from the outset by anthropologists and folklorists, ended by winning the field. Both then and now, unless we are mistaken, we have no other comprehensive interpretation of popular witchcraft; and the thesis of this English scholar, cleansed of its riskiest affirmations, seemed eminently sensible when it discerned the deformations of an ancient fertility rite in the orgies of the Sabbat. . . .

But it is not easy to demonstrate that popular witchcraft (as distinguished from generic superstition and not reducible to

a precise cult, like love philtres, spells, etc.) really goes back
to an ancient vegetation and fertility cult. A first objection has
already been expressed about Murray's work: we cannot build
uncritically upon the confessions of witches without distinguishing what part of them came from the Inquisitors, and what part
is of genuinely popular origin. But this objection is not insuper-
able. Jean Marx already noticed the existence of a group of
beliefs which, though of undeniably popular origin, nevertheless presented a certain analogy with the Witches' Sabbat
schematized by theologians and Inquisitors. More recently, Wei-
ser-Aall has emphasized the existence of this point of contact
between popular and learned witchcraft. There were beliefs,
first recorded in the tenth century but surely much older, in
mysterious nocturnal flights, especially by women, towards gatherings with no trace of diabolical presence, profanations of the
sacrament, or apostasies—gatherings presided over by a feminine deity named now Diana, now Herodias, Holda, or Perchta. The presence of goddessses associated with vegetation
like Diana or Perchta could mean that the beliefs built into
later, diabolical witchcraft are reducible to a fertility cult. The
hypothesis is more than likely, though it has not yet been
adequately demonstrated. Following this path, a German scholar,
A. Mayer, seems to me to have come closer than anyone else to
a correct view of the problem. But even his attempt, built on
slender and insufficient documentation, is basically a failure.
Moreover, one can offer him a second objection, not easy to
overcome: he, like Murray, does not explain how the witches,
priestesses of this supposed fertility cult, appear from the very
first (and not merely in later witchcraft, deformed by the
judges' presuppositions) in the guise of enemies of the harvest,
producers of tempests and hailstorms, and as causers of sterility
in men, women and animals.

Our present investigation confirms, in a zone like Friuli
where Germanic and Slavic traditions meet, the undeniable
presence at a relatively advanced date (ca. 1570) of a fertility
cult, whose adherents—the *benandanti*—present themselves as
defenders of the harvest and of the fertility of the fields. On one
side, these beliefs are connected to a larger complex of traditions
(which are in turn joined to the myths of nocturnal gatherings

presided over by feminine deities like Perchta, Holda or Diana) in an area extending from Alsace to Hesse and from Bavaria to Switzerland. On the other hand, these beliefs exist in almost identical form in Lithuania. Faced with such geographical variety, we can suppose without much risk that in antiquity these beliefs must have been spread over large parts of central Europe. Within a single century, as we shall see, the *benandanti* became witches, and their nocturnal conclaves, intended to procure fertility, were transformed into diabolical Sabbats, equipped with tempests and destruction. For Friuli, we can affirm with certainty that diabolical witchcraft was spread as a deformation of an earlier agrarian cult. Naturally, it is impossible to straightway extend this conclusion, by analogy, to other regions of Europe. Nonetheless, although partial and circumscribed, it can constitute an hypothesis for further research. From now on, the presence of this group of beliefs in a large and critical zone implies, we think, a largely new perspective for the problem of the popular origins of witchcraft.

Up to now we have spoken of the *benandanti* as a sect—a very special sect whose ceremonies, by the testimony of the members themselves, have the character of being, so to speak, purely honorary. In reality the *benandanti* spoke differently and never cast doubt on the reality of those meetings which they attended "in spirit." The attitudes of witches tried in other parts of Italy (and not just Italy) was exactly analogous. For example, consider the case of Domenica Barbarelli, a witch from Novi tried by the Modenese Inquisition in 1534. She said that "everyone wanted to go the ride of Diana, although many observed that they could not go; and . . . she was thrown into a deathlike state for about two hours, as though shut off from those around her. Upon returning to consciousness, she said these words: 'I have been there in spite of you,' and she told of several turpitudes which she said happened in that place." Here too the trip in a dream, "in spirit," is perceived as something real; for this reason the witch could make fun of the bystanders, since she, or rather her spirit, really went on the trip.

We shall discuss the significance of this travelling "in spirit" for witches and *benandanti* later. Let us begin by noting that both types affirm they have fallen into a state of profound prostration or catalepsy before going to their gatherings. No doubt [the cause of this state of catalepsy] is a marginal problem for the interpretation of witchcraft; even if we could (and we cannot) safely determine the nature of this cataleptic state, we would still need to explain the more vital significance of the visions of witches and *benandanti*. . . .

Interpretations hitherto advanced are substantially of two types: either one supposes that witches and warlocks were afflicted with epilepsy or hysteria or other nervous diseases which cannot be precisely identified; or else he attributes the loss of consciousness accompanied by hallucinations which they narrate to the actions of unguents made from narcotic or soporific substances. Let us begin by discussing the second hypothesis.

It is known that witches anointed themselves before "going" to the Sabbat. Already in the mid-fifteenth century the Spanish theologian Alfonso Tostado, commenting on Genesis, noted in passing that Spanish witches, after pronouncing certain words, rubbed themselves with ointments and fell into a deep sleep which made them insensible to fire or wounds; upon awakening, they asserted that they had gone to this or that place, even though far distant, to gatherings with other companions, banqueting and making love. A half-century later, Della Porta obtained an identical result by greasing an old woman reputed to be a witch, and later minutely listed the ingredients of the ointment used. The experiment has been repeated twice in modern times, with conflicting results: one German got a severe headache, while the other had remarkable hallucinations. Still, it seems reasonable to suppose that at least a part of the confessed witches, if not all, used ointments capable of producing states of hallucinatory delirium.

However, it is not easy to extend this hypothesis to the *benandanti*. Neither [of the first two men who voluntarily confessed to belonging to this sect] spoke a word about ointments. They only talked about deep sleep, about lethargy which made them unconscious and permitted the exit of the "spirit" from the body. Even in later trials of *benandanti* we find only two hints of this. An oxherd, Menichino, who claimed to be a *benandante* and to travel at night in the form of smoke to fight against the witches, was tried in 1591 by the Holy Office of Venice. While answering one of the typical Inquisitorial questions ("when he went out as smoke like he says, did he anoint himself first with any unguent or oil . . . or say any words?"), he at first reacted violently: "No, by the saints, God, and the Gospels, I neither anointed myself nor said any words . . ." Only during the second reading of his interrogation did he admit that the *benandante* who had first encouraged him to go out at night had told him to anoint himself "with lamp oil the evening before he went." This is a cautious and even reticent admission, which finds a none-too-solid confirmation in the testimony of a carpenter who denounced a public whore, Menica de Cremons, to the Inquisitor of Aquileia as a *benandante*, "she herself stating that when she went she anointed herself with certain oils or unguents, and that her body stayed but her spirit went away . . ." As we shall see, this is an indirect testimony and moreover a very late one (her trial was in 1626). One even begins to suspect that this hint can also be interpreted as an early clue to the assimilation of *benandanti* into witches which was occurring, as we shall see, precisely during those years. In conclusion, the testimonies about the use of ointments by *benandanti* were really too few, compared with the number of relevant trials, to accept this interpretation.

Now to the other hypothesis. It is certain that many witches were epileptics, and that many people possessed by devils were hysterical. However, there can be no doubt that we are faced with phenomena which cannot be reduced to the field of pathology: partly from statistical reasons (faced with such a large number of "sick" people, we would have to shift the boundary between sickness and health), and especially because the supposed hallucinations, although private and individual, have a precise cultural consistency—one thinks first of their occurrence within a narrowly bounded part of the year, the four times—and their contents belong to a specific form of popular religion or a special brand of deviate mysticism. The same remarks are valid for the *benandanti*. We cannot spontaneously attribute the catalepsy and the lethargy into which they fell to epileptic crises. In fact, only one *benandante*—a woman, Maria Panzone, tried first at Latisana and later at Venice by the Holy

Office in 1618-1619—suffered from the *bruto male*, or epilepsy. Of course, in her case the crises which continually beset her, even during an interrogation, could have resembled the physionomy of the ritual lethargy of the *benandanti* in specific circumstance. However, the documentation which we possess will not permit us to argue from this fact. The nature of the catalepsy of the *benandanti* remains obscure. In any case, whether they were provoked by the effects of unguents based on narcotics, or whether they were due to epileptic crises, or whether they were obtained with the aid of special ecstatic techniques, the problem of the *benandanti* and their beliefs must resolved within the boundaries of the history of popular religious beliefs, not of pharmacology or of psychiatry.

3 FROM *Emmanuel Le Roy Ladurie* *Les paysans de Languedoc*

This brief discussion of witchcraft in southern France in the sixteenth and seventeenth centuries is a tiny segment of a large book that attempts a total history of the Languedoc peasantry (over a million souls at any given moment) during a great agrarian cycle lasting from about 1450 until about 1720. Le Roy Ladurie sees witchcraft in Languedoc primarily as a form of peasant revolt. This theme is an old one in French historiography, going back to Michelet; but the particular twist that Le Roy Ladurie gives to it is novel and important. Basically, he sees witchcraft as the mythical counterpart to rural social revolts, and as a particular form of escapism which, like other rural rebellions, was incapable of assuming truly revolutionary dimensions.

SOURCE. Emmanuel Le Roy Ladurie, *Les paysans de Languedoc*, Paris: Editions S.E.V.P.E.N., 1966 pp. 407-413. Reprinted by permission of publisher and author.

Peasant consciousness is expressed authentically in popular uprisings, fiercely experienced until the final failure; but this consciousness also flowers in a mythical mode in the imaginary and fantastic revolt of the Sabbat, an attempt at diabolical escape. At the end of the sixteenth century, in effect, a diabolical wave flowed over entire regions of southern France: in the Pyrenees, in southern parts of the Massif Central, up to the Alps and the Jura. In the mountains, especially in Vivarais and the Languedoc parts of the Pyrenees, these Sabbats are contemporary with the popular revolts, or great social Sabbats, of 1580 or 1595.

Some witches were sons of peasant rebels (*croquants*): for instance the werewolf and *croqueur* Jean Grenier, son of a *croquant* and rich peasant of Coutras, condemned in 1603 by an *arrêt en robe rouge* of the Parlement of Bordeaux. As for the forces of order, tribunals and Parlements, they led the hunt for witches and the repression of the uprisings with equal energy. Finally, it is well known, thanks to the conscientious and sadistic enumerations of the demonologists of 1600, that no fact reveals more about peasant mentality than witchcraft, an agrarian movement par excellence. For instance, the lists of witches given by Boguet contain almost entirely the names of villagers, and among them a majority of women, girls, widows, shepherdesses—born conservers of rural myths.

Let us recall, in southern France, the most significant episodes of diabolical history and geography. The first among them are located at the extreme end of the fifteenth century.

About 1490, in effect, the Cévennes, just like the nearby ranges (*massifs*) of Vivarais or Queyras, began to behave like a magic mountain. In the villages overlooking Alès dozens of witches sprang up, often from specialized clans. The best-known, Martiale, from Boucoiran, passed for a child-poisoner, wine thief, and caster of spells; she had made "quit-rent" ("*censive*") homage to the Devil.

All these women are accused of celebrating the religion of the goat-devil, a "stinking and filthy beast," with its customary rites of kissing his ass, frigid embraces, dances, offerings of black candles, trampling upon the cross, and insults to the Virgin (nicknamed the Redhead, *la Rousse*). The witches are tortured and the stakes reduce them to ashes (1493).

Then the epidemic calmed down and a lasting peace began, at least locally. For the Cévennes, won by the Reformation, will abjure Satan. There at least, the Huguenots—just like Zwingli's disciples in Switzerland—succeeded in ripping the network of diabolical superstitions and in controlling the rural consciousness. About 1590, the age of the Sabbats has truly ended there. Only some benign matters—loaves of bread marked with cabbalistic insignia, magic dealings with gypsies—were censured by the Cévennes consistories. The Reformation brought a religion which was clearer, more humane, and warmer, and it effectively cured anguish (or relocated it). . . .

But this victory was partial and precarious. Partial victory: the devil, expelled from the Cévennes, kept strongholds farther north in Vivarais. There, in 1490, Louise Fumat, a peasant from St. Germain, was hanged for having trampled on the cross, prostituted her body, killed her husband and having attended the Sabbat. It was a good piece of business for her judge, Barjac, lord of Rochecolombe, who awarded himself the property of the condemned. A generation later, la Vachonne du Roux, Catherine Peyretonne, Catherine Las Hermes and others were burned (1519-1530). Their crime? They had bewitched newlyweds, spat upon the host, bewitched pigs, and danced the *gigue* around a goat.

Precarious victory: after 1550, witchcraft, momentarily calmed, resumed in a rising wave which flowed over all the South at the time of the great burnings of 1580-1600. On this subject, nothing is more striking than a comparison of the narratives of the two Platter brothers, Felix and Thomas, at forty years' distance (1556-1596). In the Montpellier region, Satanic sickness was still benign in 1556; it became serious, pathological, in 1596.

During the reign of Henri II, Felix Platter the elder, although superstitious and fearful, only mentions witches in passing: a matter of a peasant who terrifies priests, vomits flames, and dies torn apart by dogs. Felix attaches little importance to this story. In the city, the witchcraft of the 1550's is episodic, apparently linked to individual perversions like necrophagia: a witch of Montpellier, described by Rondelet, digs up the cemeteries and bites the thigh of a woman buried the day before.

Isolated cases. All in all, Felix Platter is chiefly the witness of an easy life. Forty years later, his younger brother Thomas met anguish and the fear of Satan infinitely multiplied. First the phobia of the ligature (*aiguillette*), the universal fear of Satanic castration, which Thomas describes in detail. At the moment when the priest blesses a marriage, a witch slips behind the husband, knots a thread, and throws a piece of money on the ground, while invoking the Devil. If the coin disappears, the couple will be unhappy, sterile, and adulterous: "it is beyond doubt that the Devil removes the coin and keeps it until the Last Judgment." About 1595, Platter succumbs to a full psychosis of the ligature, and his narrative, through its very exaggerations, mirrors the fears engendered by the witches: "In Languedoc, not ten weddings in a hundred are celebrated publicly in a church. Couples, accompanied by their parents, go secretly to a nearby village to receive the nuptial benediction." Only then can the newlyweds, freed from anguish, enter their home, devour the wedding feast, go to bed, and dismiss each guest with a kiss on the mouth. And Platter, a serious physician, gravely shakes his head. The panic is so bad, he concludes, that there is a local danger of depopulation, through fear of the ligature and rarity of the number of weddings!

In fact, this Languedoc drama is not isolated. In central and southern France, after the second half of the sixteenth century, from Blése to Toulouse, witches, girls, servants and even little children played the great game of bewitching the married couple, through the ligature and in fifty other ways.

The anguish of castration by the ligature is inseparable from the phobia of impotence in men, and in certain cases, of frigidity in women: the coldness (*froidure*), which Languedoc peasants of 1600 curiously associated with sterility. This theme only lost its evil powers bit by bit. Gone from Languedoc, it will survive in the folklore of Roussillon and Catalonia. And in the less-developed parts of Europe (Sicily, south Italy) young newlyweds will continue to use rituals to directly propitiate castration up to the present. The methods will be different, but the primary anguish will be the same as among the late sixteenth century people of Languedoc.

Among them, the best minds and most highly-placed people—

Joubert, a famous doctor, or Augier, *grand prévôt*—believed in deviltry and were often feared witches. Augier poisoned beautiful women with a golden jewel which contained a familiar spirit. And it was also in Languedoc, in the Toulouse region, that the two great demonologists of the end of the century, Bodin and Remy, grew up.

After 1580, with the famous diabolical epidemics (well-known in Franche-Comté and in the Basque country, where more than five hundred stakes burned), one sees the whole chain of magic mountains awaken bit by bit; great delirium factories whose chimneys again began to smoke. The power lines of demonic influence ran from the Pyrenees to the Jura, through the southern heights of the Massif Central. In the Pyrenees of Languedoc, a land of dreadful swearing, local historians were still recording, at the dawn of the Fronde, witch-trials with "spells on animals, loss of little children in the cradle, general spoiling of fruit," and in consequence, hanging, burning, whipping or banishment of the guilty parties. Farther north, Rouergue was highly infected. Around 1595, witches were ruling there over the crudeness and ignorance of the inhabitants, a rude and impious people. The men of Rouergue did not know the Bible, and since they lived in hamlets or lost corners very far from churches, they never attended Mass and were exposed to all the obsessions of the devil. Not far away, in the region of Saint-Pons, a hangout of astrologers and superstitions, the devil was equally at home. He obsessed the priest Cabrol and the notary Amblard, whose *livre de raison* for 1590-1600 preserves his anguish: with the force of six men he pulls by the feet the corpse of Suzanne Rességuière, who hanged herself at the bars of his window. And it seems to be a fact about 1605 that ghosts made the round trip from Rouergue to Saint-Pons across the slopes of the Black Mountain, sweeping the snow in front of them.

Farther east, the Huguenot Cévennes, as we have seen, no longer knew the infection except in its benign forms. The real Satanic road henceforth passed farther north. It left Rouergue and leaped over Calvinist Gevaudan to end in Vivarais. There, after fifty years of quiet, the flame of the stakes glowed once more in 1581. The magistrates, doctors and apothecaries of Annonay deployed an arsenal of exorcisms and tortures practiced in the parish churches of the town against the Sabbats of the mountain. Among the trials, we cite that of Catherine Boyaronne, aged fifty, peasant from St. Symphorien-de-Mahun: honorably-known notables of Annonay "branded her like a pig," poured boiling lard over her ears and other parts of her body, and cooked her alive, in order to make her admit that she had led her daughter to the Sabbat.

Finally, from Vivarais by way of Lyon, the demonic chain reached Savoy and the Jura of Saint-Claude, where witches swarmed in the age of master Boguet.

Those are the facts: rising obscurantism, a magical crisis at the end of the century; a rural, and particularly mountaineer, diabolism. How can it be explained, when at the same moment the Reformation seems to indicate an increase of enlightenment?

Thomas Platter proposed a geographical explanation in 1595. Where are the witches' villages, he asked himself after his travels in the south of France? Where is the Devil most powerful? And he answered, where the dispersed population, terrain, etc., prevents the peasants from attending Mass or sermons; where pastoral visitations are difficult; where ignorant rustics have no access to Scripture. Thus they are an ideal prey for the devil. Entrenched in their crannies, they secrete the agrarian ideology par excellence, witchcraft. So Rouergue, the mountain of Saint-Pons, spiritually abandoned, are nests of witches—a witchcraft of lost corners.

The explanation is too static, but it can be dynamized and inserted into the living flux of sixteenth century; for the rise in deeds of witchcraft does not correspond solely to changeless geographical conditions. It is dated, precisely situated in time. It betrays the deficiency and growing crisis of the spiritual framework. From this viewoint, some sociological analyses, though formulated in a quite different context, can, *mutatis mutandis*, bring some useful suggestions. The sixteenth-century demographic growth ended with a relative piling up of human masses in the old parishes, in the city suburbs, and on the cleared slopes of the mountains. And the local clergy, as well as the civil authorities, neither foresaw nor understood nor even noticed this phenomenon of growth. Nothing was organized to cope with it.

Only in the seventeenth century did bishops on pastoral visitations busy themselves with the sick who died alone in the crannies of recent colonization, outside all spiritual aid, far from the churches.

After 1560, the civil wars aggravated this condition of abandonment even further. Priests were massacred; others fled their insecure situation. Many ecclesiastics left their flocks, shouldered an arquebus and were made soldiers of the League. Thus clerical recruitment was poorly assured. The spiritual dereliction of the mountains, nests of guerrillas, brigandage and terrorism, was especially grievous. Far from their priests, the peasants found themselves alone, faced with their anguishes, with their ancestral terrors. They gave themselves to the devil.

Does it not, however, impoverish one's analysis to reduce the diabolical epidemic to a simple deprivation of the soul, to a devaluated conscience. even to a deficit in religious organization? Beyond this "negativity," we must restore its full and dense character to witchcraft, with its authentically rural ideological sap which runs back to the depths of time and the depths of the soul. Then it no longer seems merely the expression of a spiritual vacuum, but a lively reaction of peasant consciousness. This has been disappointed by ideologies of urban origin; after 1560, it was violated by war, haunted by poverty and death and often by sexual failure (ligature, anguish of castration) as well. All at once, it escaped, a prey to the old deliria. It gave itself to all its demons. Failing a genuine liberation, it tried the adventure of a Satanic revolt.

Between these fantastic revolts and the real popular uprisings, which both culminated in the same mountains about 1580-1600, there were geographical, chronological, and sometimes even family coincidences. But there are certain profound relationships between Sabbats and men in revolt, particularly on the level of mental structures and unconscious psychology. In speaking of the ligature, we have already noticed certain characteristic anguishes. But the very mechanisms of the makebelieve also show remarkable common traits. In both phenomena, insurrection and witchcraft, we find from time to time the schema of inversion, an extension of the dream—a fictional reversal of the real world, very common in myth-making and in "primitive thought." It is not astonishing if that inversion is linked to certain types of revolts, chimerical or effective, and often desperate. To invert the world, to turn it upside down, is not to revolutionize it, nor even truly to transform it; it is nevertheless to dispute it, deny it, proclaim disagreement with it in elementary fashion. Like the revolts, like popular festivals, the witchcraft of 1600 carries the systematic stamp of such a tendency.

Typical of this obsessional wish for changing places was the statement of a young Southern witch, a fifteen-year-old adolescent from Saint-Jean-de-Luz, describing the (so-called) Black Mass as he saw it celebrated "six or seven times" in 1609 by the priest Jean Souhardibels in a spot called Cohandia in Labourd. "At this Mass, Souhardibels performed the elevation using a black host, raised in the air with his feet up and his head down before the devil, and remained in this posture during the elevation for as long as takes to say a *credo*, and the witness put himself in the same posture before us, the better to demonstrate this to us (because Satan teaches them the most horrible tricks ever seen), and told us more—a thing which he could only express by saying that the priest's whole body was raised in the air, so that even though his body was reversed with his head down and his feet up, nevertheless during this elevation he said that the priest's body and arms were just like those of our priests when making the real elevation in the Church of God, because (the witness adds) the Devil makes all things seem reversed at the Sabbat; this seems completely impossible to men, but not to him."

Valuable testimony, for in the total absurdity of this representation—a priest who says Mass with legs in the air, face down—he shows the obstinate and finally explicit inclination of mythical thought for reversing institutions, for fanatically putting the world heels-over-head. Two years later (1611) another witness summed up the same idea in a different form, less contrary to the laws of gravity. "The priests of Labourd," he declared, celebrate a Black Mass not according to the normal rite "but all backwards;" for example, they officiate with their faces towards the people and not towards the altar as at a real Mass. Similarly, they consecrate a black coleseed in place of a white host: a tiny perversion and, as always, an inversion of normal relationships.

These themes of the "upside-down world" are not confined to the Basque mountains, that somber land of enchanters. They are found in various forms in Catalan witchcraft: Latin prayers recited backwards, demons with upside-down bodies, with faces in their abdomen (in the diabolical pictues of the Catalan school at the Perpignan museum). They can also be found throughout Mediterranean France, from Narbonne to Antibes, no longer in the drama of Sabbats and Black Masses but under the carnavalesque exterior of the Feast of Fools, of church saturnalia, of comic Masses and farcical Masses celebrated by a carnival abbot who gaily chants the burlesque hymn *Memento David sans truffe*. The bishop of Lodève, on a pastoral visitation, and the regional council of Narbonne (1609) severely condemened these buffooneries, under the same title as the ligature and the pact with the devil.

Among those who mocked the Mass and the church hierarchy, the urge for inversion went very far. A little later, Naudé will describe one of these "offices" of Mediterranean folklore at the Cordeliers of Antibes: during the Feast of Fools, cabbage-cutters, cook's helpers and gardeners move into the choir stalls in place of the authentic priests. Priestly ornaments are torn and placed upside down. Books are reversed and read backwards, with plugged glasses whose lenses have been removed and replaced with orange peels. Mass and Psalms are mumbled in small confused cries.

These themes of inversion, minutely expressed, are found not only in the saturnalia of the Sabbat and the Feast of Fools, but also in those great social saturnalias, the old-fashioned popular revolts. Lacking real possibilities, these revolts had much trouble in elaborating any effective project for the revolutionary transformation of society. When they went beyond immediate requests, they were habitually informed by a primitive—and sometimes millenarian—project for an exchange of social ranks, of reality, and of rituals: "the first shall be last."

GUIDE TO FURTHER READING

"*Any serious discussion of European witchcraft*," says the best current historian of this subject, "*must ignore the conclusions of at least two-thirds of what has been written, perhaps even three-quarters.*" (*Caro Baroja, 242*) *He continues:* "*Many of these theories have been worked out very superficiallty, and put forward more with a view to causing a sensation than anything else, to satisfy the appetite for violence of the general public.*" *His conclusions are probably not exaggerated. One of the first tasks of an honest bibiographical guide to witchcraft literature should be to warn the student that much of it is useless.* Caveat lector. *Many books on witchcraft, especially the brief general surveys of the subject, are better unread.*

General bibliographies of European witchcraft are extremely rare. In facts, no truly general guide has been attempted since the appearance of Graesse's Bibliotheca Magica et Pneumatica *in the 1840's. Two recent bibliographical guides that should be accessible to most readers are the 1140 titles of Rossell H. Robbins'* Encyclopedia of Witchcraft and Demonology *(New York, 1959), pp. 558-571 which, however, is poorly organized and not annotated; and H. C. Erik Midelfort,* "Recent Witch-Hunting Research," *in* Papers of the Bibliographical Society of America, LXII *(1968), which lists over five hundred entries on European witchcraft and related subjects published since 1940, organized under useful headings.*

The student who reads no foreign language (a considerable handicap for this subject) may acquire a general introduction to European witchcraft in the straightforward, no-nonsense narrative of the great historian of science, Lynn Thorndike: see A History of Magic and Experimental Science *(New York, 1923-1958), 8 vols., Vol. 4, Chap. 5; Vol. 6, Chap. 46; and Vol. 8, Chap. 38. He also has two recent and valuable general treatments available to him, both used in this anthology: Hugh Trevor-Roper's lengthy essay, printed in* Religion, the Reformation and Social Change *(London and New York, 1967), pp.*

90-192; and Julio Caro Baroja, The World of the Witches *(English transl., Chicago, 1964). And he has a huge mass of source materials, strewn about in chaotic fashion, available to him in Henry Charles Lea's posthumously published notes:* Materials Towards a History of Witchcraft *(Philadelphia, 1939), in three large volumes.*

Apart from these treatments, there is very little material in English bearing upon the general history of witchcraft that may be confidently recommended. There is an excellent essay by Gregory Zilboorg on The Medical Man and the Witch in the Renaissance *(Baltimore, 1935), and three valuable articles: George Rosen, "A Study of the Persecution of Witches in Europe as a Contribution to the Understanding of Mass Delusions and Psychic Epidemics,"* in Journal of Health and Human Behavior, *I (1960), pp. 200-211; John L. Teall, "Witchcraft and Calvinism in Elizabethan England,"* in Journal of the History of Ideas, *XXIII (1962), pp. 21-36; and Moody Prior, "Joseph Glanvill, Witchcraft, and 17th-century Science,"* in Modern Philology, *XXX (1932), pp. 167-193.*

There are several anthropological studies of witchcraft in non-European societies that can provide students with a valuable comparative perspective. One might begin with Bronislaw Malinowski's classic Magic, Science and Religion *(Glencoe, 1948; 1st ed., 1925); E. E. Evans-Pritchard,* Witchcraft, Oracles and Magic among the Azande *(Oxford, 1937); Clyde Kluckholm,* Navaho Witchcraft *(Boston, 1967; 1st ed., 1944); and Claude Levi-Strauss, "The Sorcerer and his Magic,"* in his Social Anthropology *(New York, 1963). There is a good up-to-date collection on* Witchcraft and Sorcery in East Africa, *edited by J. Middleton and E. H. Winter (London, 1963).*

Unfortunately, some of the best general literature on European witchcraft is not available in English translations. Included among these are Joseph Hansen's two indispensable volumes on the origins of organized witchcraft: Zauberwahn, Inquisition, und Hexenprozess im Mittelalter *(Munich-Leipzig, 1900), and* Quellen und Untersuchungen zur Geschichte des Hexenwahns und der Hexenverfolgungen im Mittelalter *(Bonn, 1901), both of which have been photomechanically reproduced in the 1960's; Nicholas Paulus' great collection of essays on Protestant and Catholic witchcraft during the Reformation,* Hexenwahn und Hexenprozess, vornehmlich im 16. Jahrhundert *(Freiburg-im-Breisgau, 1910); Lucien Febvre's brief but brilliant essay on "Sorcellerie: sottise ou révolution mentale?" in* Annales: économies, sociétés, civilisations, **III** *(1948), pp. 9-15; and Carlo Ginzburg's path-breaking monograph on* I benandanti *(Turin, 1966).*

Compared with the remarkably small amount of valuable literature on the history of witchcraft in Europe as a whole, there is a fairly large group of books and articles on the history of witchcraft and witch-trials in separate European countries. We shall list only the most important titles, grouped by nations or regions:

I. ENGLAND

1. *Wallace Notestein,* A History of Witchcraft in England from 1558 to 1718, *Washington, 1911; reprint, New York, 1968.*

2. *Cecil L'Estrange Ewen,* Witch Hunting and Witch Trials, *London, 1929.*

3. *George Lyman Kittredge,* Witchcraft in Old and New England, *Cambridge, 1929.*

II. NORTH AMERICA

1. *George L. Burr,* Narratives of the Witchcraft Cases, 1648-1706, *New York, 1914; reprint, 1952.*

2. *Marion L. Starkey,* The Devil in Massachusetts, *New York, 1949.*

3. *J. M. Taylor,* The Witchcraft Delusion in Colonial Connecticut, 1647-1697, *Grafton, Conn., 1908.*

4. *Robert-L. Séguin,* La sorcellerie au Canada francais du XVIIe au XIXe siècle, *Montreal, 1961.*

III. GERMANY

1. *W. G. Soldan and Heinrich Heppe,* Geschichte der Hexen-prozesse, *2nd. ed., Stuttgart, 1880.*

2. *Johannes Janssen,* History of the German People after the Close of the Middle Ages, *revised by L. Pastor, trans. by S. G. Middel-more, London, 1910, Vol. XVI, pp. 216-526.*

3. *Sigmund Riezler,* Geschichte der Hexenprozesse in Bayern, *Stuttgart, 1896.*

4. *Emil Pauls, "Zauberwesen und Hexenwahn am Niederrhein," in* Beitrage zur Geschichte des Niederrheins, **XIII** *(1898), pp. 134-240.*

5. *Friedrich Merzbacher,* Die Hexenprozesse in Franken, *Munich, 1957.*

IV. FRANCE

1. *Robert Mandrou*, Magistrats et sorciers en France au XVIIe siècle, *Paris, 1968.*
2. *Etienne Delcambre*, Le concept de la sorcellerie dans le duché de Lorraine au XVIe et XVIIe siècles, *3 vols., Nancy, 1949-1951.*
3. *Aldous Huxley*, The Devils of Loudun, *New York, 1952.*
4. *P. Villette, "La sorcellerie dans le nord de la France du milieu du XVe siècle à la fin du XVIIe siècle," in* Mélanges de science religieuse *XIII (1956), pp. 39-62, 129-156.*

V. SCOTLAND

1. *George Black*, A Calendar of Cases of Witchcraft in Scotland, 1510-1727, *New York, 1938.*

VI. SCANDINAVIA

1. *Jorgen Jacobsen*, Danske Domme i Troldomsager, *Kobenhavn, 1966.*
2. *E. F. Norlind, "Nyare synpunkter paa häxväsendet," in* Kyrkohistorisk Aarskrift, *XLII (1942), pp. 180-193.*

VII. AUSTRIA

1. *Fritz Byloff*, Hexenglaube und Hexenverfolgung in den Oesterreichischen Alpenländern, *Berlin-Leipzig, 1934.*

VIII. SWITZERLAND

1. *Guido Bader*, Die Hexenprozesse in der Schweiz, *Affolteren, 1945.*

IX. ITALY

1. *Giuseppe Bonomo*, Caccia alle streghe, *Palermo, 1959.*

X. SPAIN

1. *Sabestien Cirac Estopañan*, Los procesos de hechicerías en la Inquisition de Castilla la Nueva, *Madrid, 1942.*

XI. POLAND

1. *Bohdan Baranowski*, Procesy Czarnowie w Polsce w XVII i XVIII Wieku, *Lodz, 1952; summary in French.*

XII. BELGIUM

1. *Emile Brouette, La Sorcellerie dans le comté de Namur au début de l'époque modern (1509-1646), in Annales de la Société archéologique de Namur, XLVII (1954), pp. 359-420.*

Finally, it should be noted that many valuable primary sources are available in English, especially the handbooks of European demonologists translated by the indefatigable and myterious Montague Summers. He has given us the oldest and most important of them all, the Malleus Maleficarum (London, 1928; reprint 1948). He has also done such witch-fighters as Nicholas Remy of Lorraine, Demonolatry (1591; trans. 1930); Francesco Maria Guazzo of Milan, Compendium Maleficarum (1608; trans. 1929); Henri Boguet of Franche-Comté, An Examen of Witches (1602; trans. 1929); the Italian friar Ludovico Sinistrari, On Demonality (1680; trans. 1927); and Robert Bovet's Pandaemonium (1684; Summers ed., 1951), plus three lesser writings on witchcraft, including the important Confessions of the French nun Madeleine Bavent (1648; trans. 1933). The skeptical attacks on witchcraft have fared less well at the hands of modern translators and publishers; the only important exception is Hugh R. Williamson's edition of Reginald Scot's Discoverie of Witchcraft (1584: London and Carbondale, Ill., 1964). Such great classics of witchcraft literature as Weyer and Bodin have not found either editors or translators in the twentieth century.